The Book of Recruiting; Da Costa Style

By

Dean "The Tool Man" Da Costa

With

Derek "DZ" Zeller

Introduction

Hello, and welcome to the world of Dean Da Costa. You may know me by now as the tools guy. I have built, over the years, a reputation for knowing about all of the sourcing and recruiting tools out there and have been on multiple advisory boards helping guide companies and startups in the most efficient way to source and recruit candidates. I also wrote a lot of words about other subjects in the world of recruiting and this to me is just that, a compilation of thoughts I think sharing would be fun to do and a good read for you to look at and use in the future. I hope you enjoy and learn from the world I have called my home, sourcing and recruiting.

I have been thinking long and hard about writing this and other books. Thanks to the love and support of my wife Bettina and the belief of my children Jeremy and Deanna, My granddaughter Heather, as well as the support of many of my friends. I want to take this time to recognize some of the people who have been instrumental in the writing of this and the other books and in my growth as a professional. First to the ones who I learn from every day– Aaron Lintz, Steve Levy, Marvin Smith, Derek Zeller, Shally Steckerl, Amybeth Quinn, Pete Radloff, Susanna Frazier, Glenn Gutmacher, Jeremy Roberts and so many more. Thanks to all!!

Lastly, I asked Derek to help me edit this and put it together for me as we have been friends for years now and well, he is one hell of a writer so why not lean on those who can help you the most. So, thanks "DZ" you are the best.

Chapter 1

Hire Veterans

Hire Military/Veterans

"American Soldier" by Toby Keith is a song about the life of a soldier in the military, why we do it, and why it must be done. I have long been an advocate for hiring Veterans. For those of you who follow me, you may have seen my past posts on the subject or my labs at Sourcecons on Vet hiring, and you may have seen or been at my webinar on <u>Recruiting blogs</u> on Vet hiring. We're thankful this great cause has gotten even more attention as one of the greatest sourcers, and recruiters ever, Glen Cathey "<u>the Boolean Black Belt</u>" has put out a blog about "<u>How to Find Military Veterans for sourcing & Recruiting</u>". Having someone the stature of Glen Cathey means the message is getting out, and hopefully, soon everyone will understand how and why we should be looking to hire our Military Vets.

Military Staffing Series Part 1
Why Hire Military/Veterans and How to Understand Them

"God Bless the USA" by Lee Greenwood has long been the anthem for our armed forces and for Veterans. Over the years many other songs have come out reminding us to give thanks to those who risk their lives so we can live free. Over the next several blog posting I will go over why you should hire Military/Veterans, Understanding Military/Veterans, Research/Sourcing Military/Veterans and Lastly Sites for finding Military/Veterans.

First why you should hire Military/Veterans:

1). You can get between 2400-4800 in Tax Credits for hiring a Military/Veteran.
The link will take you to the US Dept. of Labor, specifically were the WOTC (Work Opportunity Tax Credit) page is and explains further about the credit for hiring a veteran as well as other guidelines.
http://www.doleta.gov/business/incentives/opptax/eligible.cfm

2). Over 200,000 service members leave the military every year.

30. Over 80% of military jobs have a civilian counterpart, meaning of the 200,000 getting out, over 160,000 will come out with skills and experience directly relevant to civilian jobs all you have to do is find and hire them.

3). Military/Veterans live by a code of Ethics, they are proven learners, they are proven to be able to work in teams, they are loyal, committed and some much more.

4). Special guideline for Military/Veterans in the USSERA - Uniformed Services Employment and Reemployment Rights Act. The link goes to the US Dept. of Labor page referencing USERRA and explains about USERRA, employer and Vet Rights on USERRA and much more. There is a USERRA Advisor which is a program

designed to help employers and employees understand their right under USERRA. http://www.dol.gov/elaws/userra.htm
5). Government sponsored education benefits, allowing a military/veteran to get additional education/training. The link provided take you to the GI Bill page. This page explains the education benefits available to Veterans. These benefits can also be used to make a veteran employable, meaning if a company needs an employee who is a veteran to get training this program can help pay for it. In the case were the GI bill is not an option Chapter 31 Vocational Rehabilitation and employment program can provide the same education benefits. http://gibill.va.gov/ And http://www.vba.va.gov/bln/vre/

In order to recruit/hire a Military/Veteran you need to understand Military/Veteran. What I mean by understanding them is understanding the terminology, and understand the jobs they had.

First, in thinking about the military you need to remember, the military is not just the Army, Air Force, Marines, and Navy. The military also includes the Reserves, National Guard and Coast Guard. http://www.todaysmilitary.com/service-branches

Within the military there are 3 levels of military personnel:
- Enlisted think of as hands-on workers or day to day operations
- Warrant Officers think of as highly technical and specialized a bridge between enlisted and Officer
- Officer the guys in charge, the high-level managers

When talking to a military person and asking them what rank they were, you may get one of 2 answers. 1 will be a letter and number designation this is really their pay grade, for example, E3. The other will be their rank, for example, PFC (an E3). For people in the military, these are often used interchangeably. For a listing of ranks see link: http://www.military-quotes.com/military-rank.htm.

Every person in the military has a MOC (Military Occupational Classification), basically their job. AS I stated earlier 80% of those have a civilian counterpart. The link here will allow you to take a military persons MOC and see what it means, and what the civilian counterpart is.
http://www.careerinfonet.org/moc/default.aspx?audience=WP

When talking with the military personnel you will hear about a DD214, this form describes a veterans type of discharge, some of their awards as well as some of the training they have taken and more. Every veteran leaving service gets one.

Another document you will hear about is PQR (PERSONNEL QUALIFICATION RECORD), this is a listing of all their training, awards, places they have serves, ranks and much more.

Lastly, you will hear about an ACE transcript, this is a document done by the American Council on Education, and will list all the training a military person has gotten, both civilian and military while on active duty and show what that training would be worth towards a degree.

I know that's a lot and trust me there is a lot more, but this gives you good foundation about why you should hire a veteran and how to understand them.

Military Staffing Series Part 2
Research/Sourcing for Military/Veterans

"Made in America" by Toby Keith is one of the newest anthems for our armed forces. In this song, he talks about how his father would pay extra for things made in the USA by people in the USA like our veterans. In this post, we are going to discuss the research and some sourcing techniques for finding veterans.

First military/Veteran search terms such as:

1). Army, Air Force, Navy, Marines, Coast Guard, National Guard, Army Reserve, Air Force Reserve, etc..

2). Organizations such as Veterans of Foreign Wars (VFW), Disabled American Veterans (DAV) etc. The link below will take you to a list of veteran and military organizations.
http://www.workworld.org/wwwebhelp/veterans_service_organizati
ons_overview.htm

3). Other words or Acronyms: Veteran, Military, USMC, USArmy, USAF, USCG, USN, Vet, Former, Retired, prior etc. See link below for a list of Military Acronyms, Initialisms, and Abbreviations.
http://www.fas.org/news/reference/lexicon/acronym.htm

4). Clearances are a huge and there are many types: Secret, Top secret, and more. Most veterans will have or had a clearance. For a list of clearances see link below.
http://securityclearancejobs.blogspot.com/2007/10/most-complete-
list-available-for.html

5). Obviously knowing the MOC and actual title used in the military that you are searching for help. So the link below takes you to the best of the MOC finders.
http://www.careerinfonet.org/moc/default.aspx?audience=WP

6). Researching government agencies can also help as many veterans may have worked for government agencies. The link below will help identify most agencies.
http://www.usa.gov/directory/federal/index.shtml

7). Also, there are a lot of companies that support government agencies (meaning companies providing talent and services to federal agencies), below is a link to a list of most of them.
http://washingtontechnology.com/toplists/top-100-lists/2012.aspx
Now with all the research done, you are ready to put together a search string. Below is a simple string that will find veterans who have Java, are ex-Army and have a Top Secret clearance.

Inurl: resume (Java OR J2EE) AND (Army OR USARMY) AND ("Top Secret" OR TS)

Keep in mind you can substitute subject and title for url and substitute bio, CV, or "curriculum vitae" for a resume. Also, you can use the pipe "|" instead of OR in Google, and you do not need to use "AND" in Google. In addition, you can use terms like –job –jobs – apply -example to remove possible job ads. You can also use the Tilda (~) instead of inurl: in google to save time.

***** Remember to do your research first*****

Military Staffing Series Part 3
Sites for finding Military/Veterans

"In America" by the Charlie Daniels Band is a song about America and its veterans. About how we may disagree amongst ourselves but when it counts we stand as one, we take care of our own. In this post we are going see the many sites that are out there, that can help us find veterans.

Monster has a special way to designate veteran candidates, and even allow us to search for veterans specifically and or to post jobs veterans will find.

First posting jobs only:
https://www.jofdav.com/
www.jobs4vets.com

Posting and sourcing:
www.jobcentral.com
http://recruitmilitary.com/
www.helmetstohardhats.org
www.VetJobs.com
www.CorporateGray.com
http://www.patriotjobs.net/

Posting, Sourcing, Programs, Information and more:
http://www.militaryconnection.com/
http://www.fedshirevets.gov/
http://www.military.com/
http://www.taonline.com/TAPOffice/
http://www.hiremilitary.com/
http://www.militaryhire.com/
http://www.hireveterans.com/
http://100000jobsmission.com/
http://www.postmilitaryemployment.com/#
https://www.rallypoint.com/

Do's, Don'ts, and some best practices:

http://nod.org/research_publications/americas_best/
http://www.americasheroesatwork.gov/forEmployers

I am constantly searching for info on finding, hiring and helping vets. The link below is to my website and specifically to the vet part so check it out for updates.
http://thesearchauthority.weebly.com/vets.html
There you have it, you now know why you should hire veterans, what you need to know to hire veterans, were to go to hire veterans and a whole lot more.

Converting a Military job to the Civilian World and More!!

One of the most difficult things to do is convert a military occupational specialty (MOS) or job to a civilian job. It is hard because the MOS's typically do not carry standard titles, and the verbiage used to describe it is military talk. The problem is without this ability you cannot help a veteran get a job, write a resume or anything. However below is a list of links to sites that can help you do this exact thing.

http://www.careerinfonet.org/moc/default.aspx?audience=WP

http://www.military.com/veteran-jobs/skills-translator/

Now prior to looking up their MOS you should also get their dd214, which is their separation paperwork and will have training and education they have received on it, also get their ACE Transcript or verification of military experience and training which will tell you even more about their education, training etc. and also get their DA form 2-1 which will have even more information about their training, assignments, and education.

Remember that in the military soldiers get a primary job and also secondary jobs and sometimes these secondary jobs are better than the primary and can open up the doors to better civilian jobs.

If you get all this it will be very easy to see what they did, how it translates to the civilian workforce and makes it much easier to help them get employment.

Veterans Specific;
Sites to Post Jobs and Search for Resumes

"In America" by the Charlie Daniels Band is a song about America and its veterans. About how we may disagree amongst ourselves but when it counts we stand as one, we take care of our own. In this post we are going see the many sites that are out there, that can help us find veterans.

Monster has a special way to designate veteran candidates, and even allow us to search for veterans specifically and or to post jobs veterans will find.

First posting jobs only:
https://www.jofdav.com/
www.jobs4vets.com

Posting and sourcing:
www.jobcentral.com
http://recruitmilitary.com/
www.helmetstohardhats.org
www.VetJobs.com
www.CorporateGray.com
http://www.patriotjobs.net/

Posting, Sourcing, Programs, Information and more:
http://www.militaryconnection.com/
http://www.fedshirevets.gov/
http://www.military.com/
http://www.taonline.com/TAPOffice/
http://www.hiremilitary.com/
http://www.militaryhire.com/
http://www.hireveterans.com/

http://100000jobsmission.com/
http://www.postmilitaryemployment.com/#
https://www.rallypoint.com/

Do's, Don'ts, and some best practices:
http://nod.org/research_publications/americas_best/
http://www.americasheroesatwork.gov/forEmployers

I am constantly searching for info on finding, hiring and helping vets. The link below is to my website and specifically to the vet part so check it out for updates.
http://thesearchauthority.weebly.com/vets.html

There you have it, you now know why you should hire veterans, what you need to know to hire veterans, were to go to hire veterans and a whole lot more.

Chapter 2

Diversity Sourcing

Diversity Sourcing 101

Diversity sourcing is a very special skill. You need to have knowledge of were to search or as I have said in my "Top Ten Rules for Successful Internet Sourcers" post, you need to do your research. Below are some keywords and phrases you can add to any Boolean search string that will increase your chances of finding diverse candidates. For the purposes of this and future posting I am focusing on; Women, Hispanic, African American, Native American. Today we will focus on Women. So on the keywords and phrases;

Women

Sororities:
Alpha Delta Pi
Alpha Gamma Delta
Alpha Omicron Pi

Alpha Phi
Chi Omega
Delta Delta Delta
Delta Gamma
Gamma Phi Beta
Kappa Alpha Theta
Kappa Delta Chi
Kappa Kappa Gamma
Pi Beta Phi
Sigma Kappa

Associations:
WITI
ACM-W
Society of Women Engineers
Association for Women in Computing
Society of Women Engineers

Other Terms:
Women*
woman*
female*
She, girl
her
Girl Scouts of America

Women's Colleges:

Agnes Scott College
Barnard College
Bennett College

Brenau University
Bryn Mawr College
Carlow College
Cedar Crest College
Chatham College
College of Saint Catherine
Columbia College
Converse College
Emmanuel College
Harford College for Women
Hollins College
Hood College
Judson College
Mary Baldwin College
Marymount College
Meredith College

Mills College
Mount Holyoke College

Mount Mary College
Mount Vernon College
Notre Dame College of Ohio
Randolph-Macon Woman's
College
Saint Joseph College
Saint Mary's College
Scripps College
Simmons College
Seton Hill College
Smith College
Spelman College
Stephens College
Stern College
Sweet Briar College
Ursuline College
Wellesley College
Wells College
Wesleyan College
William Woods University
The Women's College at the
University of Denver

Remember as I said in my "Words and Phrases to recruit by!!!" blog post, go beyond the basics. Were ever you see an abbreviation being used also spell it out, it will improve your search results.

Remember this is very easy just take your boolean search string and add on any of the above words or phrases.

example, form my "If You Build It, They Will Come: the story of a successful Boolean search string!!" blog posting, you have the below. Simply add the part in red and you have a search string that will pull up women that fit all the requirements in the string.

(title:resume OR title:CV OR title:bio OR title:homepage OR url:resume OR resume) AND NOT (job OR "career opportunity" OR "equal opportunity employer" OR "employment at" OR EOE OR "employment opportunity" OR opening OR "submit resume" OR "your resume" OR "sample resume" OR "career development" OR classified OR book OR books) AND(Cryptography OR Biometric OR Security OR firewall) AND (Symantec OR Microsoft OR Norton OR McAfee) And ("Software Engineer" OR "Software Developer" etc...) And (C++ OR C etc...) And (WITI OR "Women In Technology International")

In one of my next posting, we will look at Hispanic as our next diversity sourcing subject.

Diversity Sourcing 102

We already looked at Women so now let's focus on Hispanic. Remember Diversity sourcing is a very special skill. You need to have knowledge of were to search or as I have said in my "Top Ten Rules for Successful Internet Sourcers" post, you need to do your research. Below are some keywords and phrases you can add to any Boolean search string that will increase your chances of finding diverse candidates. For the purposes of this and future posting I am focusing on; Women, Hispanic, African American, Native American. So, on to the keywords and phrases:

Hispanic

Associations:

- National Society of Hispanic

  MBAs
- National Council of Hispanic

  Women
- Society of Mexican American
  Engineers & Scientists (MAES)

Colleges:

University of Texas— Pan American
University of Texas—El Paso
Texas A&M University— Kingsville
St. Mary's University of San Antonio
New Mexico Highlands University

Other Terms:

Spanish*

Hispanic
Latin American*
Latino*

Hispanic Fraternities/Sororities:

Gamma Alpha Omega
La Hermandad de Oe Me Te

Kappa Delta Chi

Remember as I said in my "Words and Phrases to recruit by" blog post, go beyond the basics. Were ever you see an abbreviation being used also spell it out, it will improve your search results.

Remember this is very easy just take your boolean search string and add on any of the above words or phrases.

example, form my "If You Build It, They Will Come: the story of a successful Boolean search string!!" blog posting, you have the below. Simply add the part in red and you have a search string that will pull up women that fit all the requirements in the string.

(title:resume OR title:CV OR title:bio OR title:homepage OR url:resume OR resume) AND NOT (job OR "career opportunity" OR "equal opportunity employer" OR "employment at" OR EOE OR "employment opportunity" OR opening OR "submit resume" OR "your resume" OR "sample resume" OR "career development" OR classified OR book OR books) AND(Cryptography OR Biometric OR Security OR firewall) AND (Symantec OR Microsoft OR Norton OR McAfee) And ("Software Engineer" OR "Software Developer" etc...) And (C++ OR C etc...) And (MAES OR "Society of Mexican American Engineers and Scientists")

In one of my next posting, we will look at African Americans as our next diversity sourcing subject.

Diversity Sourcing Part 202

Here is the last in the 4 part series on Diversity Sourcing. We already looked at Women, African Americans and Hispanic so now let's focus on Native American. As I said in my previous post remember diversity sourcing is a very special skill. You need to have knowledge of were to search or as I have said in my " Top Ten Rules for Successful Internet Sourcers " post, you need to do your research. Below are some keywords and phrases you can add to any boolean search string that will increase your chances of finding diverse candidates. Remember for the purposes of this posting I am focusing on; Women, Hispanic, African American, Native American. So on the keywords and phrases;

Native Americans

Associations:	Colleges:	Other Terms:
AISES (The American Indian Science & Engineering Society)	Southeastern Oklahoma State University	Indian*
		Native American*
	University of North	
SACNAS	Carolina—Pembroke	Tribe*
		Chief*
		American Indian*

Remember as I said in my "Words and Phrases to recruit by!!!" blog post, go beyond the basics. Were ever you see an abbreviation being used also spell it out, it will improve your search results.

Remember this is very easy just take your boolean search string and add on any of the above words or phrases.

example, form my "If You Build It, They Will Come: the story of a successful Boolean search string!!" blog posting, you have the below. Simply add the part in red and you have a search string that will pull up women that fit all the requirements in the string.

(title:resume OR title:CV OR title:bio OR title:homepage OR url:resume OR resume) AND NOT (job OR "career opportunity" OR "equal opportunity employer" OR "employment at" OR EOE OR "employment opportunity" OR opening OR "submit resume" OR "your resume" OR "sample resume" OR "career development" OR classified OR book OR books) AND(Cryptography OR Biometric OR Security OR firewall) AND (Symantec OR Microsoft OR Norton OR McAfee) And ("Software Engineer" OR "Software Developer" etc...) And (C++ OR C etc...) And ("AISES " OR "The American Indian Science & Engineering Society")

Chapter 3

Methodologies

Sourcing Methodology Intro

So we are going to take a break on our series on lesser sites, to start a miniseries on a Sourcing Methodology, I use that has been very successful. This will be the last post of 2017 so the series will begin in 2018, however, I will lay the groundwork here.

The Methodology is pretty simple, Research-Source-Scrape (or download), Enhance and Upload, Outreach. During this series we will break out each step in its own post, I will include what we do in that step and sites and tools to help you do it. Now keep in mind the Methodology itself will never change the only things that changes is where you do your research, where you do your sourcing, and where you do your enhancement. Now, of course, this also means the tools or sites you use might change as well.

Sourcing Methodology Part 1

Prior to the Holidays, I gave the intro to this series where we will cover a sourcing methodology. Now keep in mind this is a "Readers Digest" version, which means it is going to be short and sweet. So we will begin were all good sourcing strategies and methodologies must start – Research. The idea is to gather as much data as we can to create a Persona of the ideal candidate. Things we need will be; Salary ranges, education background, work background, the source of the candidate and anything else we think that might help.

Research falls into 2 upper categories, Internal and external. We will start with internal research. The internal research will typically be done in 2 methods; 1-data gathering from your ATS and CRM's, 2-interviews of hiring managers (HMs) and people who have or are currently in the roles (CR) and have been successful. The information you want is what we talk about earlier, Work and education backgrounds of successful candidates, the source of candidate and starting and current salaries. Now, most of this can be found via our ATS and CRM, however, the reason for talking to HMs and CRs is to get their take on everything, what they thought worked well and what worked bad. Once we have this data it is time to move on to external research.

External research is done to ensure whatever data we got from internal research still is applicable, for example, salary. Now external research has two subcategories, Industry and competitive. So let's start with industry research. What we mean here is getting the industry-specific with regards to the areas mentioned at the beginning; salaries, education background, work background, etc. These will tend to be general so you might get a salary range, or a generalized idea what kind of degree and or school people who are JAVA developers have. Some tools you can use are; Talisman, Rethinklabs, Paysa, Salaryinfo to name a few. Now comes the

Competitive intel park of the external research. This is where you get the same info as you did with the industry, but you get it from specific companies who are competitors to you, so the info will be more specific for you. Tools you can use for this are; Owler, SEC, Bloomberg, Talismatic, Insightly, rethinlabs, paysa, LinkedIn, Crowded to name a few.

Once you have all that info you can put together your Persona and enhance your JD. An example might be that after all that research you find out that the persona of the ideal candidate is; a person with a CS degree from a top 30 school and program, who worked at Amazon for at least 2 years, has a certification or 2, and is currently a Software Engineer 1, and making about 100k. Now you have a benchmark you can adjust your JD and now look at creating and or enhancing your search terms.

Well, there you have it step 1 in the Sourcing Methodology.

Sourcing Methodology Part 2 – Sourcing!!

This is part 2 of the Methodology, Sourcing. In part 1 we talked about Research, now that we have that done it's time to Source. So regardless of where you source, you need to understand one of the recruiter languages, Boolean, Symantec, and or Natural Language. Each has their place in the sourcing world.

Boolean is where it starts; it allows you to find thing son the net, x-ray into sites and more. An example string might be inurl:resume "Java Developer" "Seattle". This string is looking for the resume of people who are Java developers and are in Seattle.

Symantec is simple the resumes DB language meaning. This is how you would write a string to use in most databases, ATS, or CRMs. It is pretty simple it is the same as the Boolean minus the operators. So I string along the same lines as the one I already showed would be "Java Developer" AND "Seattle".

Natural Language is the social networks language. An example along the same lines as the first 2 using natural language would be: People who live in Seattle and are "java developers"

Now, of course, there are tools out there that can help you with writing these strings and then run them; Hiretual, Bool, CSEs, Social Talent and more.

Now there other tools that can help you source and find people such as Seekout, HiringSolved, ZenSourcer, ICwatch, to name a few.

Places to find candidates could be: Social sites (Facebook, Twitter), Conference lists, user groups, newsgroups, Code repositories (GitHub, Stack Overflow), Certification organizations, industry organizations, Company targeting, etc.

So now you have the quick and easy, down and dirty part 2, sourcing including, the languages, tools, and places.

Sourcing Methodology Part 3 – Scraping

This is part 3 of the Methodology, Sourcing. In part 2 we talked about Sourcing, now that we have that done it's time to Scrape the results.

Scraping is the act of getting the info from one source to a reusable, and mobile source such as a CSV, Txt, Excel etc. Doing this makes it easy to upload to your ATS or CRM as well as use tools to enhance the data you have.

There are many tools or methods you can use to scrape data, and we will go through some of them here.

One method is simply print screen the data and saves as a picture. However for this to work you need to be able to get the data out of the picture and put into a more usable format, such as a CSV, or Excel. One tool that you can use to do this is One Note. Simply open the print screen picture in one note, then right click and select copy data form picture and then paste into a CSV or Spreadsheet.

Another method is to copy the data by right clicking and highlighting the data and then copying it and pasting into a CSV or Excel or Word. Now, this method can be easy but the data usually comes out in a unorganized way.

Lastly, you can use a scraping tool such as Dataminer, Instant Scraper, Scrape Similar, and many others. Most of these have a Chrome Extension as well. They all will scrape the info you want and produce a very well organized excel or CSV version of the data that is ready to be enhanced or uploaded.

So now you have the quick and easy, down and dirty part 3, sourcing including several methods to scrape.

Sourcing Methodology Part 4 – Enhancement

This is part 4 of the Methodology, Enhancement. In part 3 we talked about Scraping, now that we have that done it's time to Enhance the results.

For the purposes of this methodology, Enhancement means finding more info, such as; emails, phone, social sites, etc. Obviously, there are many methods of enhancement. For example a boolean string "person's name" (email | phone | Cell | contact) will find some of the data that qualifies as an enhancement.

Of course, there are a plethora of tools that can do this as well. Tools such as Hiretual, Seekout, Toofr, Loxo, Blockspring, knowem, and many, many more. In some cases, this is a one at a time thing. In others, it is a CSV upload. Either way, you can enhance the list so that they can become viable candidates. Once they are all enhanced you simply upload to your ATS or CRM and you're on to the final step

So now you have the quick and easy, down and dirty part 4, Enhancement. Including several tools.

Sourcing Methodology Part 5 – Outreach!!

This is part 5 of the Methodology, Outreach. In part 4 we talked about Enhancement, now that we have that done, and of course uploaded our list to our ATS or CRM, it's time to reach out.

This has 2 parts; 1- creating a good message/email, 2- methodology of reaching out. First, there is creating the messaging. There are tools that can help you create an email that will get you a high response rate this mail can also be used on Linkedin. These tools can help you avoid spam, cultural issues, readability issues and more.

- First up is Textio. Textio is a tool that uses advanced AI to determine just how good of an email or message it is so, the higher the score the better.

- Next up is Readability-Score. This tool will give you the readability level of your email. You need to watch for both the normal readability and the automated readability as a lot of people use things like Alexa or Cortana to read their emails. Optimally you want an 8th-grade normal reading level and 6th-grade auto reading level.

- Now for the engagement level, this shows how engaging your email is. For this, we use MosaicTrack and their AI based engagement measuring tool.

- Now for issues such as Cultural, Sexism etc. so for this, we use Joblint and their AI based Issues tool.

Lastly, we deal with Spam. This is where a lot of people lose. To help with this we use Melon-stork Spam tool, any grade less than 5 is good, the lower the better.
Now we have our email it's time to send it. Below is a good plan for not just emailing but calling, SMS, and social contacting.

1.   Day 1 email – the first contact should be email
2.   Day 2 – take a break day to allow them to digest, presuming they did not reply right away.
3.   Day 3 call – the second contact should be over the phone with a follow up on other Social media methods and, follow up +SMS/Text (80% of texts are read).
4.   Day 4 – take a break day
5.   Then repeat the entire process a minimum of 3-5 times, before moving the candidate to a once a monthly follow up or stopping. However the callings part repeats it up to 8 times, but no more than 2 times in one day.

At some point, if you want to add to your email you will call the next day that is okay but does not do it on the first go round.

Sourcing Methodology Conclusion!!

Over the last several weeks we have covered all the parts of the "Sourcing Methodology". We went over a boatload of tools, all of which can help you do your jobs.

Tools such as Owler, SEC, Bloomberg, Talismatic, Insightly, rethinlabs, paysa, LinkedIn, Crowded for research. Hiretual, Bool, CSEs, Social Talent, Seekout, HiringSolved, ZenSourcer, ICwatch for sourcing. as Dataminer, Instant Scraper, Scrape Similar for scraping. Hiretual, Seekout, Toofr, Loxo, Blockspring, knowem for enhancement and Textio, mosaic track and others for outreach. We even went over an outreach methodology. You now have a good, solid methodology for sourcing and outreach and are ready to go. As new tools become known such as Whoknows (a sourcing and enhancement tool) you will know right where they belong.

Bdbdbd! That's all folks!

Chapter 4

Getting the "MOST" Out of Yourself!

"MOST"-Part 1

The 4 pillars needed to get to the next level.

Often I am asked what the secrets to my success are. When I try to explain it, most people thought some of these secrets were not something you could learn, you either had it or not. To a point this is true, but also to a point you can learn them and as such can get better.

So here I will identify the pillars, and then in the following 4 posts, I will further explain the pillars and what they give you. In the last post, post 6, I will show how they connect and how you can gain them and thus allow you to get the "MOST" out of yourself as a staffing professional.

- Pillar 1, multitasking, the ability to do more than one thing at the same time, that is one of the most important things. When most people hear the word multitask they think 2-3 things at once. However, in my world, it could mean as many as 15+ things at once or more.
- Pillar 2 Organization, you need to be organized to the point you do not waste time looking for information or trying to remember what search goes were etc.
- Pillar 3 Speed, not just fast but warped speed fast, the ability to perform at warped speed is essential to the pillars.
- Pillar 4 Time Management and planning, simply put you need to understand or learn how to manage your time effectively and have a plan.

Together these 4 pillars make up the "Most" technique, a set of skills needed to get you to the next level.

"MOST"-Part 2

Multitasking!!

So this is part #2, pillar 1 on the "MOST" technique.

Pillar 1 is multitasking, and the ability to do more than one thing at the same time. When most people hear the word multitask they think 2-3 things at once. However, in my world, it could mean as many as 15+ things at once or more.

For the purposes of this post we are going to call any activity we are performing a process. So in my case I have 8 computers and when I am working I usually have all 8 going and each performing at least 2-5 processes each, and I bounce from process to process. I mean let's remember if the process we are performing is a search there are what I call down times within the process. A downtime would be the time after you have put in your search parameters and enter a search. There is usually a few seconds of downtime before the search results are pulled up, why wait, move on and get another process started.

Now I understand not everyone has 8 computers, but the idea works with even 1 computer, just use multiple windows and have multiple processes going at once. In other words "Multitask".

As I said in earlier posts all the pillars are interconnected. So while 10+ processes seem like allot, and you might worry about keeping it all straight and QC, if you use and learn all 4 pillars you will have no problem handling more processes than you would have thought. Of course, this is another one of those learned but cannot be learned, as you can learn to multitask to a point but without some inherent ability you will be capped. I cannot guarantee everyone will handle 15+ at once, but if you learn and use all the pillars you will handle more than you can now.

"MOST"-Part 3!!!

Organization!!

So this is part #3, pillar 2 on the "MOST" technique.

Pillar 2 Organization, you need to be organized to the point you do not waste time looking for information or trying to remember what search goes were etc.

The organization is a very important pillar to the "MOST" technique. If you are organized, your ability to multitask will go up. You can learn organization skills in very many places but one of the best is yourself.

That is right yourself, one thing we all need to remember is all the training in the world on the organization will only go so far. You need to learn how to implement these skills within the confines of your own abilities and ways of thinking.

Remember to take advantage of your natural born abilities when applying any organizational skills you pick up. For that matter whenever you learn any skill or techniques always see how you can utilize your natural born abilities to enhance what you learned.

"MOST"-Part 4!!!

Speed!!

So this is part #4, pillar 3 on the "MOST" technique.

Pillar 3 Speed, not just fast but warped speed fast, the ability to perform at warped speed is essential to the pillars.

So this is a biggy, speed can be god given, or gained over time and effort or both. For our purposes, we are talking work speed.

So gaining speed can be done in a lot of ways. If you learn to type faster you will increase your work speed, if you learn to think quicker you will increase your work speed if you are better organized and know where all the info is you will find it quicker. All of these things will increase your work speed.

As with all the pillars they are interdependent. Also as with multitasking, you can increase yours with training and practice, but it will only go so far some of it will be inherent.

"MOST"-Part 5!!!

Time Management and Planning!!

So this is part #5, pillar 4 on the "MOST" technique.

Pillar 4 Time Management and Planning, simply put you need to understand or learn how to manage your time effectively and have a plan.

Time management and Planning are together because if you have a plan you will manage your time correctly if you managed your time correctly you had a plan even if you did not know it.

So this is another skill that you can learn. There are many ways and thoughts on how to manage your time. I prefer utilizing a PM style of time management.

That being to utilize a schedule to lay out what I need to do and when I need to do it. Also having a plan for what I am doing.

An example you are scheduled for sourcing, something that should be on your schedule every day, you have 30 openings to source for. That's great but if you do not have a plan, that meaning what positions to source for, how many candidates you want to find etc., you will waste a lot of time on 1 or 2 positions and end up not having any time for the others.

Now you can see how Time Management and Planning go together and how they all fit with the other pillars.

"MOST"-Part 6!!!

Bringing it all Together!!

So this is part #6, Bringing it all Together with the "MOST" technique.

Okay so let's bring it all together.

If we learn how to multitask, then we can get more done in a short time frame, which will help with time management and planning and be helped by being organized.

If we are organized, we will be able to work with more speed as we will know where all the info is, and we will be able to make a good plan that will allow us to multitask and manage our time correctly.

If we can learn to work with great speed, we can get more done in less time, and to do this we must be organized to easily and quickly find info.

If we learn to manage our time and have a plan we will be able to work with great speed and multitask.

Notice all the repeated words; notice how they all overlap from pillar to pillar. That is what I meant by interdependent. Each pillar needs the other to form a strong foundation that will allow us to get the "MOST" out of ourselves as staffing professionals.

Now we can learn to multitask and increase our ability to multitask with practice, but again only to a point at some point, some will be able to multi-task more than others because it is just inherent.

You can learn to be organized in fact most PM courses teach you organization, and there are a lot of books, and courses on it.

You can gain speed in allot of ways, you can learn to read faster, you can train your mind to think quicker, as you do more and more you will gain speed it is just human nature the more you do something the quicker you will get with it. Of course, training and experience will only take you so far like with multitasking some of it will just be inherent.

You can learn Time Management and Planning. In fact, most PM sources cover this and there are numerous books and courses on the subjects.

Now for the quick plan:

Take a PM course and take what you learn about time management and planning and being organized and use your inherent skills and abilities to come up with your way to get the "MOST" out of yourself as a staffing professional and keep with it. The more you do it the quicker you will get with it, the quicker you will work and the more processes you will be able to handle as you learn to be able to multitask at a greater rate.

I have always said the biggest difference between me and others is speed, multitasking, Time management and planning, organization and research. I have already posted numerous posts on research, and things related to that such as thinking out of the box, not settling for the easy and simple things, etc. Now with the conclusion of the series on "MOST" you have the things, abilities, and skills that allowed me great success.

Interviewing

Lookology

Lookology is the second half, along with lisology, of an exciting and innovative new screening and interviewing methodology called Looklisology.

Lookology is the advanced art of utilizing nonverbal communication in interviewing, sales meetings, and more.

Non-Verbal Communication is defined as communication that does not involve speaking. Lookology takes it to the next level and takes into account all types of nonverbal communication and the information that can be learned from it.

Lookology takes into account; hand gestures, posture, eye contact and motion, subtle changes in facial expressions or skin tone, head angle when talking and listening, and numerous other nonverbal cues, that the body will give that can tell you allot.

It is allotted lot like giving a tell in poker. Most tells are nonverbal. In interviewing you can use the same principles to learn when someone is telling the truth or not. Also, when they are really listening, when they really care, it will show and so much more.

One thing to take into account with regards to Lookology is culture. In some cultures, certain nonverbal communication tells are considered the norm as opposed to a true tell.

At the end of the day, Lookology can be a great tool for interviewing candidates. Couple it with Lisology and you have a complete toolbox of interviewing skills, I call Looklisology (Look (Lookology) and Listen (Lisology) that will greatly increase your success as an interviewer.

Lisology

What is Lisology? Lisology is one half of an exciting and innovative new screening and interviewing methodology called Lisology. Lisology is the art of not just hearing what is said but listening to what it said, how it is said, the words used, the way they are put together to form answers or phrases, the inflection in peoples voices, the stutters, the silence, the emotion or lack thereof behind what is said, what is not said and more. Think of it as "Active Listening" on steroids.

Active listening is defined as, intentionally focusing on who you are listening to, whether in a group or one-on-one, in order to understand what he or she is saying. As the listener, you should then be able to repeat back in your own words what they have said to their satisfaction. This does not mean you agree with, but rather understand, what they are saying. Now Lisology takes it to a whole new level and incorporates, not just hearing what is said but hearing what is not said.

With Lisology you can determine so many different things. You can determine the strength of conviction by not just what is said, but the way it is said, the words used to say it. If someone says something in a strong tone, which oozes confidence they probably have a strong conviction about the subject. If they choose their words quickly but correctly they also show strong conviction and understanding of the issue or question asked. If they choose their words quickly but incorrectly they are probably trying to fool you and you need to probe further.

These are just examples of how Lisology can be a great tool for not just recruiters but anyone doing interviews or business development. If used right you can plan your whole interview around the information you gather from Lisology. Every answer can lead down a new course of questions to determine the information needed to determine whether or not this person is the right candidate. Lisology works best in determining soft skills, business skills, and general fit for a position and organization. However, it can be used for any type of interview.

Lookology equals "What Every Body is Saying" by Joe Navarro

Lookology was the opposite of lisology and part of the looklisology interviewing process. Both are interviewing techniques, both are designed to take interviewing to the next level, and work very well with behavioral interviewing. Lisology was the process of not only listening to what is said but the way it is said, the choice of words, inflections, pauses and sighs to garner more information about a candidate. As you can imagine Lookology is the process where we look at the nonverbal communication going on during an interview. These nonverbal communications are also called "tells". Well, A friend of mine was telling me about this book called, "What Every Body is Saying" by Joe Navarro. I bought the book and read it, in fact, I am rereading it. This book sums up lookology and in fact teaches it in a way, better than I ever could. In this book, Joe makes it clear how to identify all the things I talked about in my blog on Lookology. Joe takes his 25 years of experience as an FBI agent, an expert in "Speed-Reading" people and explains to everyone how you can do it, and in my blog, I explain how to use in interviewing. It's a must-read, if you want to be a better interviewer and expert in Lookology.

The BTOS Interviewing System

The premise behind the BTOS (Business, Targeted, Open Door, Sequential Interviewing system) is utilizing behavioral interviewing and Looklisology (see previous blog posting on Looklisology) and Probing questioning to combine and form a unique, highly flexible, and successful interviewing system. To start let's look at the definitions of each of the main parts of BTOS

Business Behavioral Interviewing(BBI)- Business Behavioral interviewing has a specific style and approach. This approach relies on the use of open-ended questions versus closed questions that require a simple yes or no answer. Business Behavioral Questions provide interviewers with a pattern of behavior, business/soft skills (negotiating skills, problem-solving, communication etc..), evidence to judge a candidate's ability to perform within the companies culture and general business style and approach. Most of these fall under general skills that most all employees should have, regardless of job function. You can also use this type of interviewing question to assess fit within a group or organization.

Targeted Behavioral Interviewing(TBI)- Targeted Behavioral Interviewing style questions that are geared toward technical/specific job/function skill areas, "Tell me about a time you had to design a website?", of course, out of this, you will move into Open Door and Sequential interviewing. Remember the whole BTOS system is connected. One thing will always lead to another.

Open Door Interviewing- this is where you utilization of your Looklisology skills, pay off the most, in noticing parts of an answer to a question that should be probed further i.e. you ask a question about an uncomfortable situation, and you notice when giving a part of the answer the person seems to get uncomfortable, this opens the door for you to probe further all the while doing so utilizing a BBI, TBI or Probing style.

Sequential Interviewing- this is simply when you take the next logical step in questioning anyone. Example if you ask them to tell you a time when they had to build a website, one of the next questions to ask in the sequence might be, what tools, languages etc.. did you use. These sequential questions do not have to be TBI or BBI type questions but more of the Probing style.

Probing style interview questions- These style of questions are much more direct and not behaviorally based at all. These questions are used primarily in Open Door or Sequential interviewing. These questions are designed to get specific information from a person i.e.. "What tools did you use in designing the website". This style can be used on technical skills, general business skills and at any time where you need a specific non-behaviorally based answer. More just than just facts.

Example:

Targeted Behavioral interviewing (job specific or technical) - "Tell me about a time you had to design a website?" which leads to…

Sequential interviewing - "What tools did you use?" (Using Probing question)-" or "Tell me about the tools you used, and how you used them? "Tell me what others on the project did etc." (TBI or BBI) which leads to…

Open Door interviewing-were you notice the candidate got visibly uncomfortable talking about what others may have done on the project. This leads back to TBI, BBI or Probing Interviewing and

"tell me how the project team worked and got along?" (TBI or BBI)
"Where there any team members difficult to deal with?" (Probing)

See the whole method is connected and works together to provide a complete interviewing system. In fact, some of the questions you ask may cross boundaries as to what type they are. They could be a combination of TBI, BBI, and Probing. You can almost only have one or two questions ready and because of the methods described here, you will end up with many more that will give you a clear picture of this candidate and what they can do. Whether you start with BBI or TBI, you will at some point hear an open door or see a sequence of questions that must be asked, and at some point require a clear-cut factual answer to a required probing question.

Sometimes utilizing just one way of doing things or system does not work. You need to utilize more than one. When that is the case remember BTOS is such a rich system that you can utilize any one part of it and with a simple modification create a system that works just for you. For example, you can use less TBI and BBI and more probing questioning, or only BBI or only TBI. This is a mix and match system. But as I said, in the end, the system will help ensure you are making the right hiring choices.

Chapter 5

Recruiting Musings

A Vision, A Revelation

Recently I was at a Symposium, here in Seattle, WA. It was being run by the people from Abrita and specifically Shally Steckerl, who I have known for some time. At some point in the symposium the subject of what are we, as staffing professionals all about. I do not recall exactly how it came about, whether someone actually said this, or enough things were said to lead me to this "revelation", but somehow I came away with an epiphany of sorts. What exactly are we, as staffing professionals really all about?

The conclusion I came up with, or the vision I had was simply, (again not sure if this was actually said, alluded to, or somehow it just hit me) we are about **"Helping people connect with their destiny's"**. Think about this for a minute. Whether it is helping the candidate find the perfect job, or the company finds the perfect candidate. We are helping them find their destinies. Those places were at that point in time they belong.

So given this "revelation", I have made it my vision statement. I want to "Help people to connect with their destiny. I want that "win-win" scenario that only happens when the destiny of employer and candidate intersect. Even if only temporarily.

So given this, we as staffing professionals are not simply in the business of hiring and filling positions, but of aligning the destinies of employer and candidate to form the ultimate win-win scenario, or as I call it the "The Utopian Effect". Think of it as the mythical, when the stars align and all is right in the world. In this case, it is the destinies of candidate and employer aligning. This event can happen frequently if the hiring manager and staffing professional are aligned to form a "hiring team" (see blog title "Bring the Hiring Manager Closer to Staffing (HMCS) Methodology") and will also be the ultimate reward for any staffing professional.

USCM, and What it Does

This is an updated version of this process. USCM stand for "URL and web page Source Code Manipulation and study." Basically, it is the practice of looking at the URL of a web page or the source code to either change it to get access to new things or study it to find and pull out information. It consists of 4 processes;

1: Peeling Back
2: ASA (Addition by Subtraction by Addition),
3: AMC (addition to Making a Change),
4: Study.

Let's start with the URL. URL stands for Uniform Resource Locator. Basically the address for the thing you want to see. Whenever you search for anything on the internet, and you go to a specific page, in the URL window will be the URL of the page. The interesting thing about the URL is what can be found by manipulating it. With "peeling back", you see what info a particular URL brings and you peel back part of it to see what else there is. For example (these are made up examples) you might see a URL that is; http:www.lockout.com/profile/a/developer. This URL might bring back a page of someone in that company who has a profile and their name starts with A and is a developer.

With "peeling back" you might take away everything after profile to see what happens. Sometimes this will yield a directory or pages were all the profiles of the company are listed. Sometimes it will do nothing. With ASA you might remove the developer and replace it with the architect, hoping to get architect resumes that start with A. With AMC you would simply change the A to B, and in most cases, you would get all the developers whose name starts with B.

So "peeling back" is just removing to uncover new info, ASA is removing some and putting in new, and AMC is simply changing a part of the URL, to show more data. They are all related but do different things. To say it another way "peeling back" is removing, ASA is replacing, and AMC is changing, and the whole process is USCM.

A real-world example would be the URL below:
https://www.linkedin.com/company/cisco/followers?page_num=1&trk=extra_biz_followers

The URL above is the url for all the people on LinkedIn who are following Cisco. Now in looking at it, the first thing I see is where is the word Cisco and I was wondering what would have happened if I replace Cisco with say Boeing. Guess what that change now makes the URL show all the people on LinkedIn following Boeing. That is AMC.

For the purposes of the next part of USCM, specifically "source code", we will be talking about Internet Explorer and the 4th process Study. So every browser has a way to view the code behind the page you are seeing. A lot of great info can glean from that code. As it relates to LinkedIn sometimes a personal email address might be listed in the source code, Links to the location of pictures will be listed there, links to other pages and so much more. If someone has their own personal page, but does not show an email address, but does have a way to contact them, if you Study the source code sometimes the actual email address will be there. All you have to do is look. The way you look is to go into going into view and then press source, now remember this is in IE, in Chrome, you go into tools and view source.

The key with USCM is your ability to observe, think, study, make logical conclusions, and manipulate what you see. There you have it USCM, and what it can do for you, if you take the time to look, study.

Background Checks do they really work???

Background Checks are a must for me. They help you validate someone's work history, education, and criminal record. Of course, you can also validate their credit score and more, but the work history, education, and criminal record are the biggies.

The key is to ensure you use a reputable service and remember that no matter what the result is you need to use it as a piece to a puzzle, not as a deciding factor.

Background check s can be wrong, they can say someone does not have a degree when they really do, or even that their work history does not check out. The key is too always allow the person you are doing the check on to answer any concerns. They may have all the proof you need to validate their work history or education.

As with recommendations and references, background checks should be used as a piece of the puzzle.

Analysis Paralysis!!

Over the last few months, I have posted numerous posts about staffing matrixes. The main point was to not over analyze or get so caught up in the different stats and matrixes that you forget the who, what , when , how and why of the numbers. Well, there is another potential problem with having too many matrixes that is "Analysis Paralysis". Meaning you have so much info that you have no clue where to start. Worse the info contradicts each other. Remember stats and numbers can be made to show whatever you want. For every stat that shows a problem, there is one showing there is not. When you get so immersed in matrixes, and stats that you are not sure what to do you have essentially entered a state of paralysis, and you end of stuck. Hence why I always say simple is better. Utilizing simple matrixes designed to only find the most important stats and then finding out the, who, what, when, how and why of the numbers, help you to steer clear of "Analysis Paralysis".

Using 5H&W is the Key to Everything

The 5H&W stands for; who, what, when, where, how and why. If we are doing things right these 6 words are always used, will always provide the information and answers we need and are the key to success.

For example, doing research prior to sourcing is centrally the key component. When doing this research you should, as a minimum be asking the following questions;

- Who would have these kinds of skills, who might know people with these skills
- What are these skills used for, cloud security? What other names or acronyms might these skills go by?
- When are they used, frontend, backend etc?
- Where are they used, what companies, what locations etc.
- How are they used, what operating systems (OS) etc?
- Why do these skills go together, why do they work with this OS, why are they used etc.

Now, these same 6 words can be used in any situation and will help be a guide for things to do and ask to help us do our jobs. Another example of the intake meeting, where we meet the hiring manager (HM) to discuss the new opening. Things we should ask as a minimum are

- Who is currently doing this job, who should be on the phone screen
- What will this person be working on, are they have to have skills, nice to have
- When do we need it filled by, when can you do phone screens
- Where does it need to be located, where do you recommend we look
- How often do you want to have update meetings
- Why are we looking

So as you can see if you keep in mind the 5W&H rule you will always have a plan, always have a basis for your questions, for answers you need for just about anything.

Making it Easy to Apply

Over the last few weeks, I have gone out to many company sites and check out the style, process, and length of time to apply for an open position. I was amazed at some of the things I saw. About 50% of the companies·had easy, quick ways to apply, took less than 5 minutes. Another 20-30% took 10 minutes or less. However, up to 30 % took over 10 minutes with some as much as 25 minutes.

What started me down this was when a recruiter friend of mine had told me how he does not get many applies when he posts his positions on the company site. I knew from experience he wrote great job descriptions so I knew it was not that. So the question was what was it. So I went to the site and started the applies process, 20 minutes later I was done and for me it became obvious.

I then decided to do a little survey; I spoke to about 40 people who were currently looking for work. I asked if they would take the time to apply for a job if it took 15+ minutes. 98% said no. that was huge. I asked why and it was obvious, it took too long, made them wonder if it took this long to simply apply, how long would it take to hear anything if at all, how long would the process be, and if to apply was so long, so cumbersome, what was it like to work there, how serious about finding people are they.

Well, there you have it, for those companies who have never bothered to check how long the application process is, you may be losing some great candidates and not even know it. You may be getting a bad rap, all because you apply process is way too long, As I have said many times, simple is best. Make it simple, allow them to upload a resume, and have the system take the info from the resume, and fill out any forms needed. Then all the candidate needs to do is verify the info, and apply. Simple, quick, and it works.

Be a Free Thinker

Be a free thinker. Stop looking for something wrong and look for something right. For some reason it has become prevalent for staffing professionals (SP) and hiring managers (HM) to look at resumes and candidates trying to find something wrong, trying to find a reason not to talk. Here is an idea try something new, becomes a free thinker, instead of looking for something wrong look for something right. Find a reason to talk to them; you will be surprised a resume or profile only says so much, it is only designed to say talk to me, for all too many HMs and SPs use it as a reason to say no, they look for reasons to say no. Stop. Look for reasons to say yes, find a reason to talk to someone and I guarantee you will find it increases your hires.

Chapter 6

Staffing Musings

Little Words that can Change the way we Communicate

There have been numerous books written on the subject of communication. One of the best is "Conscious Business" by Fred Kofman. I am reading this book now, but have read numerous others on the subject. There is one thing that sticks in my mind and that has been how the littlest words, can have the biggest impact on communication and the ramifications.

We as human beings like to use the words, they, he OR she, it, that, those, etc.. All of these words are used in explaining why something that went wrong, failed, or did not happen was not our faults. Why it was something or someone else's fault. These words are depowering words. However, we as humans do not like having culpability when things go wrong. We prefer being able to put the blame elsewhere rather than deal with our failures. It is human nature.

The reality is we should be using words such as **I, We, Me, Us**, etc.. When explaining why things went wrong, or did not happen, or failed. These words are empowering words. The reality is in every scenario where things did not go right, there were things that we could have done, said, not done or not said that would have changed the outcome. In other words, we have culpability for those failed events. The sooner we realize this and adjust our behavior accordingly, especially with regards to communication, the sooner we can empower ourselves to become better.

Let's think about it for a second. Let's say you and a coworker are working on a project together. You meet to go over the project just before it is done. Let's say for the sake of the discussion, you coworker forgot 1 line of code, and because of this the code is not working and the project could fail. If you communicate with them using the "you" word, they will hear that as you blaming them, and pointing fingers. This will result in a bad work relationship, and the strong possibility the error will never get fixed, as it is very likely you will get into a quarrel about whose fault it is, as your coworker will defend themselves against what they perceive as an attack, where you are blaming them.

Now let's say you meet with your coworker, you realize there is a missing line of code, but you also realize that it is as much your fault as theirs (this will be true in 99.9% of the cases. Anytime there is an outcome, in any event, everyone involved in the event, directly and indirectly, will have culpability, good or bad). So you use the word "we", as in we have a problem, you maybe even use the word "I", as in I messed up and did not see this earlier. Now all of a sudden your coworker realizes that you are taking responsibility for a mistake which may or may not be your fault. They are much more open to finding a solution. In most cases, they will also want to take responsibility for the mistake. In the end, you will worry less about the whom of the mistake, then just fixing it. I can also tell you your coworker will have a much higher opinion of you, and so will your other coworkers and your boss.

This skill, the ability to use words that show you understand how your actions and inactions can have a negative impact on events, the ability to recognize them and to verbally express this understanding, can be used in solving problems.

It is really simple, the disempowering words create an adversarial situation that solves nothing, while the empowering words create a team situation, which solves problems, creates better working relationships, and gets things done.

When Administrivia gets in the way!!

We all know there is a requirement for a certain amount of administrivia as a staffing professional. Whether it is; writing to contact a candidate, writing a job description, or writing up your interview notes, there will always be some administrivia.

However, there comes a point when administrivia becomes counterproductive and even hurts morale. Usually, this comes in the form of reports. For some reason, we in the staffing world, get inundated with reports. Now some reports make sense; hire reports, total number reports, etc.. Some make no sense, and end up eating up more work time then they are worth.

We have all seen these types of reports, they provide information, that is irrelevant and or are usually a line item report, that requires a way too much info, and time. These types of reports are a type of micromanaging. An example is a line item screen report. This is a report that shows how many candidates a recruiter spoke to in a given week. Usually, there is some matrix attached to it, saying you must talk to X number each week, of course, this matrix is in addition to the X number of hires a month. Usually, the report requires you to not just provide a number, but the names, the position you spoke to them about, the outcome, etc.. The reason for this is, there is a belief that the number of screens done, correlates to submittals, which correlates to hire. To a point, this is correct, to a point. But let's remember, without sourced candidates, there are no screenings being done, and therefore no submittals, and no hires. If recruiters are spending upwards of 40%(see below) of their time filling outline item reports, guess what suffers first? You got it for sourcing. Now if this can be done automatically through an ATS or HRIS system great, but all too often it cannot and the recruiter pays for it.

First, the idea that you have to keep track of this information, in a line item type of report, is ridiculous, in that filling out the report takes up way too much time. Now I am not saying that knowing this information is not a good thing, although I would be more interested in sourced and submitted candidate numbers, than screened candidates. What I am saying is if you want this information make it simpler. Why not just a total number of screened candidates, total number sourced, totally submitted, total interviewed, and total hired. This would take less than 10 minutes to provide, it is a simple email, and appointment count. Rather than the several hours, a line item report would take. Of course, remember this is only one example of counterproductive administrivia, I am sure there are plenty of other examples that might even be worse.

I remember in one of my positions there was a group that had to supply line item reports on screens, and they had to have X screens a week, and X hires a month. Those recruiters had to work twice as hard and barely made their number each week and month. A large part of that was because 40% of their time was spent doing administrivia related to these reports. Another group during that same time only had to report on the total number of sourced resumes, number of screens, number of interviews, number of hires. So they had to supply more numbers, but because the information was totaled, not line items, it took less than 10% of their time. Because of this they not only made their goals but exceeded them by an average of 50%.

In one of my next blog posting, I will talk about matrixes and the different ways we goal recruiters. But for now, the point of this is to be careful that you do not tie your recruiters up with counterproductive or useless administrivia so much so, that they cannot do their jobs.

Rumor and Innuendo can Destroy a Career; #truestory

Yup, it is true, it does not matter how good the facts say you are, how good the stats say you are, all that matters is what the "in crowd" "the click" think. It can even be an out and out lie, but if that group of people who are on the "in" think it is true, or propagate it, you are done. Even if you are the top performer in the company the world will come after you.

It is scary to think that in companies. Managers would rather just make the "in" crowd happy then find out the truth, or stand up to them. It has gotten so bad, that the "in" crowd, which usually consists of a bunch of average performers who have managed to stay in a particular company for a while because they are good at being fake and phony, can actually determine everything. Now, what really causes this is a bunch of weak managers, who would rather just get rid of the "target" of the "in" group, then actually do the right thing, and stop the silly stuff. But do not be fooled into thinking the "in" crowd or as I call them the "click" do not know what they are doing. In most cases, it is very calculated and is designed to target someone who is performing better than them, or maybe who they think is getting paid more than them. Basically, the target is getting or doing something the click, feels they cannot do or should be getting, and rather than learning how to do it, or working harder to get whatever it is they think they should get. They would rather find ways to alienate those that do get it.

So what to do, that is a good question, the best thing to do is to try your best to get along, and allow your success to stay between you and your manager. Believe me, this will not guarantee anything. If they cannot find anything based on fact to cause trouble with, they will just make it up. The only sure fire way to not have this happen to you is to ensure you have a strong manager and support system.

The moral of the story is, be careful, there is always a click in every company, and all you can do is the best you can and hope you have a strong manager to support you. Remember the more successful you are the more of a target you will become. Everyone wants to knock down the top dog. Some do it the right way with hard work; others try to do it the wrong way. It will be your strength, the strength of your manager and the company that will determine the outcome. So make better choices.

Bring the Hiring Manager Closer to Staffing (HMCS) Methodology

The idea behind MHCS is one of training, informing and creating a true, collaborative "hiring Team" out of the hiring manager, recruiter, and interviewers. This method blurs the corporate lines of demarcation that exists between these function to create a truly unique and highly agile and successful "Hiring Team". Some of what will be accomplished are:

1. A better understanding by the Hiring Managers (HM) and their teams of staffing.
2. A reduced time to fill, due to better communication and a more collaborative environment.
3. The ability to be flexible and maximize resources available within the Hiring team (HT).
4. So much more.

Now keep in mind this method is not needed in all cases. This method is best used when you have a client group that has a history (not a good one) with staffing or has a high number of openings. Basically what we are going to do, is put more responsibility, whether implied, perceived or factual on the HM and HT for staffing. People tend to react much better when they have a vested interest in things. Now I know some of you are saying well, it's in their opening? Isn't that vested enough? No, as long as there is, that clear line of demarcation, meaning as long as there is a clear separation between recruiter and HM they do not have enough of a vested interested. As soon as they see the recruiter, interviewers, and HM as an HT, then they are vested enough. Also in most cases, the HM is usually the biggest roadblock mainly due to them only having so many hours in a day. By introducing the concept of HT, you alleviate this and give the HM a chance to allow their people to grow by being more involved in staffing.

The whole method came about as a direct result of the realization I had that most HMs really do not get or understand. Recruiting (See my blog on the subject). If they understood more and understood what it really takes, they would have a greater appreciation and be more willing partners.

**Huge key to this whole method is consistent, 2 ways, respectful, "Conscious Business" communication. No egos, no hubris, no hidden agendas.

So the Methodology itself is really very simple, and some of you may already do parts of it.

1) First instead of waiting for a HM to write a JD or using a JD already written, when you hear of an opening, or as part of a regular check in with your client group/s, arrange a meeting with the HM to discuss the opening and the JD (If the HM already has a JD, review it with them and move on). **Spend time with him looking at JDs from competitors that you find on the internet by doing research (the same as sourcing only in this case looking for a JD). You do the research together because it allows you to get a better feel for what the HM is really looking for, and for the HM to get an idea of your capabilities around researching or sourcing and writing JDs as well as competitive intelligence and salary info. Make sure the JD is current, exciting and sure to grab candidates attention (again see my blog posting on the subject of JDs)

Once you have created a good, solid, agreed upon JD (or modified one already made), you are ready to move onto further info. Now the following is a list of additional info you should gather from the HM. This will show him you know what questions to ask and you are genuinely interested in filling the opening, of course, this is not all-inclusive and you can add or subtract from it.

- Competitors who may have people doing this kind of work?
- Who is doing the work now (reason to see their resume as a model?)
- Tradeoffs, you already have a JD worth needs, nice to have, etc. Ask if there are any tradeoffs. This will get him to think even more about what he might be looking for.

- Who might he/she or any of his/her people know (referrals)?
- Buzzwords, any particular buzz words to look for.
- What is a day in the life for this position?
- Salary range
- Specific questions the HM thinks should be asked

Now that you have asked the questions, go into the process. Make sure the HM buys into the process as you outline it, if not find a happy medium that all can agree on, but will still accomplish the results. Do not get bogged down in administrivia. Allot of times the process is never fully outlined and as such there are misunderstandings. If need goes so far as to create an SLA(Service Level Agreement), but ensure it is a 2 way SLA(meaning it states what both parties agree to) and be sure the HM buys into it and even helps write it. Include things like turnaround time on resumes, interviews, Regularly scheduled staffing meetings or attending staff meetings and having staffing as part of the agenda and communications. Try to have the HM commit to a 24 hour turnaround time or less. If need be you can even show the time it takes using the current process and how much quicker it would be with this process (use MS Project to show this). Show the interview to offer ratio using the old process as compared to the new process. This is key to the process, as most SLA around staffing involves what staffing will do for the HM. However, with this process, the SLA is a true agreement about expectations from both sides, which by definition, blurs the line to create one SLA of what the HT will do.

Ask who will review candidates? Remind the HM it does not have to be them, that it is ok to delegate, and that you can train anyone who needs it. Identify who will be on the formal interview loop, technical interviewers etc. At this point, you can now identify and explain who the HT is to the HM and make him understand how this will help in making a great hire as quickly as possible.

Now if you are dealing with a huge team, and multiple HMs who are looking for the same thing, you introduce the idea of the "Recruiting Ambassador). This is an alternating position (meaning it changes every month or so), that acts as the spokesperson for the entire group on matters related to staffing.

Now it is time to source.

This is very important and is a major key for this process to work

You want to source with the HM the first time so they see what it is really like to source and be a recruiter. This will make them better understand how difficult it can be, and allow them a better appreciation of recruiting. This will also let them see examples of what is out there, and in most cases resonates with the HM about other things they may or may not want in a candidate. As a result of this, the JD may be modified, and expectations may be changed. Now if you are not on site with your HM and HT you can still do it utilizing various sources, such as; Goto Meeting, Webex, live meeting and more.

You can also, this is huge, set up regular HT sourcing times (in addition to regularly scheduled staffing meetings), where you make yourself available to a source with the HM or other members of the HT. The key is you have already gotten the HM to understand the HT concept and that they do not need to do it all themselves. This is big as it helps show the HT you are serious, shows them the "love" and the candidates you find during this time are already one step farther than the ones you find on your own since the HT was there and already likes what they see from the resumes.

Were this process saves time is by establishing up front how the process will work, and ensuring all parties truly understand what it really takes to make a successful HT. It opens an avenue for the HT to actually be proactive about filling their positions and allows for a true partnership. If everyone understands, buys in on it, then there is more committed to it and things happen faster.

Now as I said earlier, some of this you may already be doing, but I am betting few are doing it all. Remember communication is key and ensuring the HM understands and buys into the concept of the HT is also crucial.

** Key part to the method**

Total Staffing Optimization(TSO)

Total Staffing Optimization (TSO), is the optimization of the job description, resume(where appropriate), website, and staff so that they are easily found when doing internet searches. Basically, it is Search Engine Optimization (SEO) for Staffing.

Definitions

SEO – This is short for search engine optimization, the process of increasing the number of visitors to a Web site by ranking high in the search results of a search engine.

TSO - Short for Total Staffing optimization, the process of increasing the number of visitors to a staffing or company jobs page. Also, a process by which we increase the likely hood of a job description or resume will be pulled in a typical internet, HRIS or ATS search.

Company Job Site: Obviously since a company's job site is very important to staffing it would need to be optimized. For this, you can utilize standard SEO methodology. To do this many factors come into account (this is not all inclusive):

1. Key/Buzzwords
2. Links
3. Tags, Meta tags
4. URLs, Domains, Misc

To help you with this I am providing some links to tools I find very helpful. Some of them can help you with the other parts of TSO below.

http://www.webseoanalytics.com/free/
http://websitehelpers.com/seo/

http://www.smallbusinesssem.com/how-to-seo-your-site-in-less-than-60-minutes/593/

Now some of the things they talk about are advance. However if you focus on; Keywords, and tags you will accomplish allot.

Resume Optimization- The idea is to ensure your resume or the resume of the candidate, whether on the web, in an ATS/HRIS system or where ever, has the greatest chance of being pulled by a recruiter or company or the hiring manager. You do this by ensuring you have all the correct keywords or as they are called "Buzz Words". There are several methods to make this happen:

1. **Job Descriptions (JD)-** look at the JD of the positions you are submitting for, make note of the key, job-related words used. Make note of the words that are used allot. Look at other JDs of similar positions and do the same. Soon you will have a list of "Key or Buzz Words". Also ensure you pay attention to titles, as each company may call a particular job by a different title. I know a company that calls its PMs, Account Managers. You need to ensure the resume has as many of the relevant words and titles as you can to ensure you have the highest chance of being found.

2. **Thesaurus-** Yes that is right a thesaurus. Because so many companies use so many different words in describing a job or position you must be prepared for them all. A simple check in a thesaurus can help you see if you missed anything. If you are a PM look it up in a thesaurus see what other words also mean PM, I can guarantee you some company or recruiter will use it.

3. **Dictionaries-** Technical and non-technical- These come in handy, in that acronyms, and names of things change, get added to constantly. Be sure to use an online one, since they will be kept up to date the most and be cheaper.

4. Do research on the company, you find what is their culture and way of doing things and that will tell you the kinds of words and phrases they will look for

The key with a resume and the biggest tool is the JD, this is the key as it says what that company wants. You may, in fact, have to perform this process multiple times for different jobs and JDs.

Job Description (JD) - This is where the rubber hits the pavement for staffing. A good JD means everything. Ensure you JD takes into account all the varying words and phrases that might be being used by candidates who would be a fit. For example, do not write and post a JD for a recruiter and not have the words staffing, sourcing, and recruiting, etc. in it. When candidates search they might miss your JD because they searched understaffing and your JD did not have it. If the need has at the bottom a tag area where you put such tags in. As I said in my blog post" How to write a great job description", Buzz Words are key to a great JD.

Social Media- Now a day's everyone has a blog, or tweets, or whatever. When doing so and doing it in a staffing (work) capacity ensure your posts have the needed tags to get maximum visibility. It does you no good to post if no one can find your posts. If you have a professional social media persona, where you talk about your company, yourself as a staffing professional also ensure you use the right tags and buzzwords. Make sure you are professional. Google yourself see what come up, ensure you add yourself to places like; wefollow, zoominfo etc.

Company News Propagating (CNP)- Big phrase. Basically, it means setting up news feeds (RSS- Really Simple Syndication) from Google or other sources, which come to you in your inbox. Taking the ones that help you and your company and sending them and the link out via social media, utilizing the correct tags. I have set up numerous feeds, which come to me via email, coming from Google, and other such sites, about different companies I have worked for. I read the emails and send out, the good ones, via, twitter, LinkedIn, Facebook, and other Social media; I use the right tags and buzzwords. This helps to bring your company and yourself into the forefront of people minds and this can lead to connections and candidates, but most of all great PR for you and your company.

Staffing News Propagating (SNP) - Like CNP(but not company orientated) the idea is to get you as a staffing professional out there and known. This will lead to people following you and as a result, lead to connections and candidates. You can set up feeds to you of staffing related events, news, tools, etc. and then propagate them out. Ensure you are using the right tags, buzz/keywords etc. This will help people see you and by proxy your company, as in the know about things and worth keeping track of.

The key to remember is all these tricks, and tools work professionally and personally. Also, remember while this sounds like a lot of work to set up and maintain, there are tools out there that can make it automatic requiring little work or upkeep. Tools such as; Ping.fm, hootsuite, tweetdeck, yoono, twitter feed etc..

Well there you have it; TSO, in all its glory. However, if you re-read it all you will notice the heart and soul of TSO or any internet or database optimization is; Key Words, tags, and Buzz Words. If you ensure you have enough of them and they are appropriate then you will be found.

Sourcing in a Panic! But Why?

The latest in the LI User Agreement/ToS and its anti-add-on saga has people sharing a list of add-ons that LI is *supposedly* monitoring. The reason I'm using *supposedly* is that no definitive proof has been offered confirming such a dastardly surveillance program.

That said, I do believe such a monitoring program exists and that the list is accurate (in fact, there is even a Chrome extension called Nefarious that will tell you which extensions LI is monitoring). It should also be noted that *monitoring* does not necessarily mean *you're going to the LinkedIn pokey*; it only means that in several instances LinkedIn likely doesn't know how a particular extension interacts with their platform and is hoping to *catch it in the act*.

The core problem is that these articles are titled using the following statement or some variation of it: "List of Prohibited LinkedIn Plugins". In reality, when you read the hyperlinked article the author admits, *"We cannot say that these extensions are illegal"*. In other words, they don't know yet the title and accompanying article serves one purpose: *To shock and elicit fear.*

Perhaps you noticed that Connectifier – owned by LinkedIn – is on the abovementioned list. This in itself should have served as a soothing cup of tea to calm your skittish Sourcing senses. Further, of all the people I've heard of who got in trouble with LI in recent months, most were for sending too many InMails that were either declined or the recipient said they did not know the person. Digging deeper, it was discovered that there were a few *jailing incidents* that supposedly involved extensions but only two specific extensions were mentioned (my attorneys urged me to not mention these): 2 out of the 100s that work on LI. Hardly sounds like something to cause a Sourcing breakdown, right?

Finally, let's remember that while there are 500 million *registered members* on LI there are over *2 Billion* on Facebook – and most of these add-ons work fabulously well on this other social site. In other words, take a breath, step away from the ledge, and remember LI is not the end-all, be-all for Sourcing great people.

As of now it is not definitively known what is or is not allowed and likely never will why never? Because companies have funny ways of working with each other that's why. That said, here is a quick yet not all-inclusive set of rules for using an extension with LinkedIn:

...if the add-on requires permissions to access LI, it is probably not good.

...if the add-on covers up a decent size part of the LI User Interface, it is probably not good.

...if the add-on scrapes LI quickly or views too many profiles in a short period of time, it is, well, probably not good.

Again, these guidelines are not all-inclusive and there are exceptions – and of course, LI can change their minds at any time. There's one more item to be concerned about – some of these add-ons also have an extension: While an extension might be in question while working within the LI UI, its functionality remains while working within the add-on's own workspace.

While this issue is being played out in real-time by LI sheriffs, keep yourself informed by following related threads on various Facebook groups (such as Sourcecon) about sourcing and read what is being said by the "industry leaders" and those that might have received "LI summons" and make your best-informed decision as to which tools to use and which ones to retire.

The Dumbing Down of Staffing!

That's right; I said it, "The dumbing down of Staffing". As much as we all love technology and tools, I mean one of my monikers is "the Tool Guy", technology and tools are dumbing us down. What I mean by that is we have a breed of staffing professional, that all they know is checking their ATS, checking the Monsters, Dices, CareerBuilder's, etc., and that's all. Even a lot of our experienced professionals are relying so much on tools and technology they have forgotten how to do their job without the tools and technology. How to do their job without paying for these tools, they have forgotten the basics of staffing, part of which is thinking. I was thinking about all the variables, thinking about a complete sourcing plan, and thinking outside the box. When those things run out or fail they're done. Heck as a whole I am finding a lot of staffing professionals forgetting about how we used to do things and do it for free.

Do not get me wrong, I know tools, I use tools, but I also use what made staffing great, the old school tried and true techniques that many staffing professionals have forgotten. Things like x-raying, peeling back, ASA, Boolean, doing your research first, thinking outside the box, hunting, and so much more (I call these "the staffing building blocks" (SBB)). I recently was talking to a few staffing professionals, I started talking about some of the techniques I mentioned above, and while they heard about them, and could even perform some little simple searches using these techniques, they really did not understand how they worked or just how much you could do with them. They did not understand how you could use zip codes in google to ensure your results were from a specific geo. They did not know you could source for people in LinkedIn without having a LinkedIn account.

Obviously, I was amazed, but they explained we have tools that can do all of that for us, and do it quicker. I asked them if they had any openings they have not been able to find someone for. I got 1 person saying yes; it was a very specific, security developer with a particular background. So I said let's all look, right now. They all used their tools, and I used the old school techniques. When we were done we compared results, in the end, I found everyone they had found and about 30% more, and while I took about 5 minutes longer, given I found significantly more, and it was free, the extra time was not an issue. We then looked at them all, I had all the ones they did, and of the 30% I found they did not, 90% were on the mark, with the other 10% were really really close. The difference was I did my research and was able to search places they did not, using SBB. They were amazed and what started as a simple meeting, turned into a full-on training session on SBB. I even showed to their wide amazement how to find work emails for people for free, and validate they were correct for free. The reason I specify for free is there are now tools you can pay for that will do this for you, well all of it except validate it. I tested them I was as fast and that included the validation.

Added to a dumbing down on our sourcing skills, comes a dumbing down of our research skills. I asked and was amazed at how few of the staffing professionals I was speaking to, actually did any research about what they were looking for before they started. Most all said, why waste time, when the JD says most of it, and the tools will find it all. I said really and asked a simple question, give me the words you would use to find a "java" person. All I want was the relevant words for "Java". Pretty much all I got was Java. After having everyone do about 5 minutes of research, they found out a whole bunch of other terms they should be using.

However this "dumbing down" is not just about sourcing or researching, it is about candidate engagement. These same groups of staffing professionals, pretty much do not pick up the phone, or use texting. They email, or Inmail if LinkedIn, but that all. I was like really, you do not think after sending an email you might follow up with a text or call the next day? They did not understand that emails can get trapped in junk folders, or not even get there. I simply explained to them if the candidate was good enough to send an email they should be good enough to call or text and doing so would increase their response rate. Of course I explained to them not to use the standard we have a job for you, but instead get creative.

Staying on the telephone, I asked if anyone ever tries to put together org charts for companies. They all said yes and I asked how? As I expected they all said using sites like Cogmap. I asked what they do when they get all that those sites have and they still do not have everything they need. The answer was "nothing". I asked why not call into these companies, why not try to use your telephone skills, combined with the info you have to see If you can get someone to tell you more? Why not use Boolean to try and find more info. The reaction was a dumbfounded look of, I did not know you could or how to do that. That's when it became obvious that "The dumbing down of Staffing" is well on its way to becoming an epidemic, one that can only be solved with training on the basics of staffing, and sourcing.

I am not saying you do not use technology or tools. What I am saying is overlay those tools, with the basics of staffing and sourcing. It is something that a lot of staffing professionals right now do not or, cannot do. The way you can use these tools, and the results you can get would dramatically increase if you understood the basics.

"The Dumbing down of Staffing" is here, and is happening, and only those who remember to use and or take the time to learn the basics will survive and truly flourish and be worthy of calling themselves "Staffing Professionals".

The Methodology to Make Sense of the Madness

So last week I wrote about how some seem to feel the usage of tools in staffing and sourcing is unneeded. I went on to explain why they are wrong and said I would layout my methodology for determining which tool to use and when.

So as a preface I would hope you all have taken the time to learn the "Building Blocks" of staffing and sourcing that I outlined in the previous blog titled "The Method to the Madness".

Now this blog is not going to be a full-on all-inclusive methodology, This is only going to be relevant to the use of tools I mean tools I am excluding an ATS/CRM

Now the method! First, you need to understand that all tools, extension, apps, etc. fall into categories. The categories include:

ATS/CRM, Boolean tool (BT), Search/Sourcing tools (SST), Scrapers (S)People Aggregators (PA), Contact finders (CF), Engagers (E), Timesavers (TS), Email (EM), Maintenance (MC), Security (SC), Misc (M), etc.

Now as to a methodology, my methodology is a bye product of experience and knowledge. There is no full proof methodology because there is too many variables. What might work for 1 person looking for IT industry people might not work for another looking for Energy industry people. However, my methodology is tied very closely to the Staffing Life Cycle

For me, I always start with research and out of that research the tools I need to use become obvious. A simple methodology is:

- BT to create a Boolean string
- SST to find candidates
- S to scrape info
- PG to find more info
- CF to find more contact info if needed

- E to create and implement an engagement strategy
- TS these are tools that can help implement your engagement strategies or other things quicker. These will include auto searches, mailing list, email scheduling etc.
- Now which tool form each category do you want to use, that is a matter of preference, requirements, and availability.

If I am a new staffing professional I would use Sourcehub (BT) to create my string, and then use that string in Linkedin (SST), Data Scraper (S) to scrape the info and any results would also have results in Prophet (PA), and if need be(this would mean my people aggregator did not find any contact info) use "Find that Lead" (CF). Then I would use Crystal (E) to help me craft a good email and then use my email program to send it. If I wanted to send my email at a specific time and since I use Outlook (EM), I would use Outlooks ability to schedule my email (TS) and as part of my email allow them to schedule a time to talk with me using "Schedule Once" (TS)

What I also did was create a spreadsheet with all my tools broken down by category and subcategory. I also made sure there is a column for notes, such as only works on Linkedin or if they can do multiple things, etc.. At first, there was no order to them, but over time as I have found which ones I use the most they get put into an order based on that exact thing. I even used color codes.

Now, this is really simple, but you get the idea it is really simple and goes right in line with the Staffing Life Cycle. Over time you will determine which tools form which categories work best for you. Some of that might be done for you as tools evolve, go away or no longer work well.
That's it

Words and Phrases to Recruit by; in no Particular Order

These are my seven go top I use as a sort of a methodology to makes sure I am both efficient AND that I can find what it is I am looking for. You can modify this in the future but I think it is a good set of bones to start with for sure.

1. **Take control!!-** This means to come in and establish yourself with your client. You must establish credibility, in order for them to truly work with you and for you to have the type of presence needed to be viewed as the "Recruiting Master" and SME.

2. **Establish Process!!-** Make sure you establish the process you will use to help your client fill positions. A well established and agreed upon process make it easier all around. Everyone knows what to expect from you and what is expected of them. Go so far as to create an SLA or SOW even.

3. **Go beyond the Basics!!-** This means to go more than the minimum. If looking for a VB person do not just search under VB, spell it out Visual basic. Find out more about it and see if there are other names or acronyms that can be used for it. Is it part of a bigger product? Find out more about the JD, really understand it. Maybe even go so far as to shadow someone doing that job for a few hours. Get a copy of a resume of someone who is doing it now and really doing well. When searching does not just use "resume" use CV, Curriculum Vitae, Bio, Profile. Do not just search in a paid site and that is all. Utilize all the search and recruiting sources available(I will be listing some at a later post). In other words, do not just do what is easiest or is basic recruiting. Do more, go above and beyond.

4. **Over-Communicate!!-** As with any relationship, communication is key. I have found it is far better to over communicate than under communicate. Clients appreciate knowing what is going on and one of the biggest complaints about recruiting is lack of communication. One of the biggest ways to do this is to manage your inbox. Do not let it become overwhelming and a place where emails go to die. Stay

on top of it. Create rules and alerts to help deal with some of the emails and see #6 below.

5. **Warp Speed!!-** This means simply work fats, work like it is important because it probably is. Do not procrastinate and put things off. You will find that usually when you do, things creep back up on you and you run out of time. So work is "Warp Speed", meaning work as fast as you can while not giving up quality. Trust me your clients will appreciate it and you will find it gives you more time later.

6. **Multi-Task!!-** This simply means to do more than one thing at a time. Do not just source on the internet for one particular job, when you could have several windows open, sourcing in multiple places, for multiple jobs. Learn how to do more than one thing at a time, and you will find you have more time for those emergencies that always come up.

7. **Organization and Planning are the glue!!-** This is by far the most important one of all. You must know how to organize and plan your time effectively. As an example, one of the biggest problem recruiters have is finding time to source. This is most true of corporate recruiters who get sucked into all sorts of things. Well simply put sourcing time on your calendar for every day. This guarantees you time to source. But do not just stop there. Go in with a plan. Know your openings and have them prioritized. Set a number of candidates you want to find for a given opening on a weekly basis. Do your sourcing at the time you set forth, but follow your plan. If you have 50 openings, and you have decided 5 for each a week is good, Then use your sourcing time to find your 5 candidates for the first opening and then move on to the next. This ensures you will find candidates for all your openings, and usually will leave you some time left. Most recruiters I know when they do source get so caught up in one opening, by the time their sourcing time is done, they have only sourced for one opening and have numerous more they have done nothing with.

All of these words or phrases will help you be a better recruiter. As you can see they all connect in some way. So if you do them all you will excel. But of course, keep in mind. These are not the only ones. These are just the ones that I have found have served me the best

Top Ten Rules for Successful Internet Sourcers

Every experienced Internet Sourcer uses a general list of guidelines that they work successfully by. Like any profession, Internet Sourcers have a "Rules of the Road" that assists them in finding qualified candidates. These rules are not necessarily in order of significance since I find them all equally important in your Internet journey.

1. **Research Comes First** – Every great Sourcer should have an organized library of resources. Whether this comes in the form of organized bookmarks and favorites or a notebook, it is imperative to track your research. Sourcers also understand the necessity of tracking their research and search strings using research forms. My research form includes synonyms to keywords, a list of competitors and their URL's, as well as association sites and universities that offer the particular discipline among other things. I have a research folder in my favorites that include subfolders for associations, company profile information, company financial profile information, industry resource folders broken down by discipline as well as news resources and a variety of other links.

2. **Homepages ARE Resumes** – I can't stress how important it is for Recruiters to think out of the box when it comes to Internet research. For instance, if I found the homepage of a candidate who listed their interests as java programming and has links to several java sites do you think I can consider them for my possible java developer opening? Of course! The same goes for most homepages you run into. They don't always have a full resume listing their experience etc. Sometimes you have to do a little more digging to form a lot more subtle of clues.

3. **Always Use the Advanced Search Function When Available** – Since you are an advanced Sourcer, you should always use the advanced services when available on a search engine or other directory or look-up. Have prepared Boolean

search strings ready for each type of advanced search in a search engine so you only need to cut and paste your position specifics. You should have a listing of industry-specific search strings which include x-raying, peeling, ASA and flip searching every url of each industry competitor and having this in cut and paste form so you are not always reinventing your power search string.

4. **No Access, No Problem** – A good Sourcer knows that just because you are not allowed access to a page, does not mean you can't still get in. If you can't get in the front door of the site, then backdoor the server by using the advanced function on a search engine. You can do this relatively easy by x-raying the server. X-ray allows you to ask a search engine for every web page on a server. Many times companies will have pages on their server that are not linked to any of their main pages. Search engines still index those pages so they may be able to pull them up for you. All you need to do is go to the advanced search function on most search engines and type in host:thesite.com AND the words you expect to find on your no access page. It never ceases to amaze me how often companies give all of the information on several of their key employees directly on their site.

5. **Always look at the URL** – Too many times we click to a page that has some of what we want but not all and thus we hit our back button and continue on. A good Sourcer always reviews the URL of the page to see if they can peel back each subfolder to find what else is on the site or using the ASA method add to or substitute in the URL to gain access to more things. Many times behind a resume page is a directory of other similar resumes or an additional page that explains a lot more about the candidate in who's resume you are reviewing. Don't miss out on this crucial information! Simply take off the last portion of the url that occurs after the / sign and finds these pages that are a wealth of information. In fact, most of my searching involves peeling back from the search engine results to find the true nuggets of what I need!

6. **No Contact Information, No Problem** – Many sources on the Internet will list names but not contact information of potential candidates. You see this many times in press releases or when x-raying a company server. A good sourcer knows this is not a problem. If the name is unusual like mine you can find out more about your "potential" candidate by simply going to a meta-search engine and typing in the name within quotes. If you've already determined that the candidate is someone you definitely want to talk to then find the contact information is easy. First, check the worldwide yellow pages by going to **www.worldpages.com** and typing in your candidate's name. If you would like to get email information, my favorite is **www.theultimates.com**, which will meta-search many of the main email look-ups for you.

7. **Executive Searching is Easiest on the Internet** – The Internet has really turned this field around in the sense that any good Sourcer rejoices when having to source high-level executives because they are the easiest to find on the Internet. Tremendous sources for finding high-level executives are company profile sites list like **www.edgar-online.com** or **www.herring.com**. These sites will many times list out the executives at each organization, as well as their title and in many cases their salary! Once you have a name, it's not a problem to find a bit more about your candidate by meta-searching and then find the contact information (see above). Yes, we Sourcers love searching for Executives because they are very public figures and thus are all over the Internet!

8. **Don't Stop at One Search Engine** – Do you know which search engine is the largest, meaning it indexes the most of the World Wide Web? Most would probably guess Google and would be very wrong. Search engines are wonderful things, but the problem is that none of them have indexed even half of the Internet. This means if you enter a search into AltaVista and get zero results, this may not be the case if you go to Hotbot or Google. Each search engine indexes the web differently, searches the web differently and thus has

very different results. A good Sourcer knows that they should be searching for a few search engines before exhausting the search. Many of us become pros at one search engine and stop there. A successful Sourcer is a pro at a few search engines and knows how to use them inside and out. In addition, there are "meta search engines" (MSEs)that search several search engines at once. They can even search internationally and utilize your Boolean search string creation skills you gain from my "If you build it, They Will Come: the Story of a successful Boolean Search staring!!" blog posting, you will be in a great place to take advantage of all they can do. A great Sourcer will know how to use search engines and MSEs inside out.

9. **A Good Sourcer Knows When to Use What For Best Results** – There are plenty of people who know how to Flip Search, X-ray, Peel back, ASA etc.(see earlier blog postings) There are very few people who know when it is best to use which technique. I also see people mix up the techniques so that they are x-raying a company server as well as asking for "resumes" in their search string! It is very important to not only understand each technique but WHY and WHEN you would use it. Truly successful Sourcers not only have a strong knowledge of the various techniques, but they know exactly which technique to try first for the best results. This takes a strong understanding of recruiting in general, as well as the ability to break down a requisition, understand its parts and what is most important to source for.

10. **Go beyond the Basics** - If you have read my earlier blog on Words and Phrases to Recruit by!!! , You know what this means and its definition can be extended to include not giving up. Good Sourcers do not know the words give up or quit. They are relentless hunters, who never say die and never retreat or surrender and most importantly never give up on a search. Why? Because with over 200 million pages on the Internet and over 20 million resume/homepages/bios. etc. they know the odds are in their favor that they will find the

candidates they need. A successful Sourcer knows that regardless of how good they are, it still takes quite a bit of time to successfully source all over the Internet.

Looking for Predetermined Responses can Cost you Candidates

Throughout my career, there is one thing I have noticed out of novice recruiters, interviewers, HR personnel, companies who are young or inexperienced in hiring and recruiting and hiring managers. That is the "predetermined response". The predetermined response is the response the person asking the questions wants to hear. Anything but this is not good to the person asking the question and in most cases will disqualify the candidate from contention. This phenomenon is most prevalent when the person asking the questions is using a script or questionnaire.

There are several negative connotations that come from this phenomenon, first, you come off as being very rigid, closed-minded, incompetent, and in some cases dumb. Secondly, you lose a lot of very good candidates. Coming across dumb, incompetent, closed-minded, and rigid, hurts both your name and the company you work for. While you might think there are so many candidates, it will not get out, and or no one will care, you should check out glassdoor (http://www.glassdoor.com/index.htm) and then tell me if you still believe no one will find out or it will not matter.

As to losing good candidates, the reality is, that there is always more than one correct way to answer a question correctly. If indeed the interviewing is being done properly, you are using Behavioral Interviewing, BTOS (http://www.recruitingblogs.com/profiles/blogs/the-btos-interviewing-system), or some other standardized interviewing style or technique, and you will not be looking for a standard or predetermined response, and you already know what I just said. However, if you are not, and you are looking for a standard or predetermined response, then you will lose good candidates.

Companies say they want people who are smart, innovative and think outside of the box. If this is true why would you want or expect a standard or predetermined response? What you want is the off the cuff, inventive answer.

So the moral is, do not interview anyone with any expectations of what you want to hear. Instead observe, and listen. You do these two things, called Lookology and Lisology or Looklisology (http://www.recruitingblogs.com/profiles/blogs/lisology-1 and http://www.recruitingblogs.com/profiles/blogs/lookology-1) and you will not lose out on any good candidates, and also make you and your company look good.

Hiring Manager Wanting to Hire From a Resume

Believe it or not, there are hiring managers (HM) who want to be able to make a hiring decision from a resume. They may not admit it, but deep down, that is what they want. Mainly it is because they do not want to commit the needed time to do it right. As a result, allot of great candidates get passed by, and jobs that should be filled relatively quickly take forever.

How do we stop this, is the more interesting issue. Sometimes the only way to stop it is to explain to them what the resume is really for. As most of us know a resume is not designed to say "hire me". It is designed to say "talk to me". Sometimes an HM needs that explained to them. Sometimes he even needs it proved to them. The best way to do this is to get resumes of really good people currently on the team and show the resumes to the HM so they see what you mean. You can even take the names off to further prove the point. You would be surprised how well this can work.

In the end, it is all about educating your HM about staffing and how it really works as opposed to how they want it to work.

Good Recruiters are Empathic

Yes, Empathic, the ability to sense or feel others emotions, and motivations. A good recruiter has gained this ability.

It goes hand in hand with Looklisology (http://www.recruitingblogs.com/profiles/blogs/lisology-1 and http://www.recruitingblogs.com/profiles/blogs/lookology-1).

The ability to sense what someone is feeling, or what is motivating them, is not some sort of ESP. It simply the logical, thought process was we take the visual and audible clues that everyone will give when responding to questions. Sort of like a tell in poker, these clues will tell us a lot about the person. And it is more than just what they say and does and how they say and do it, but what they do not say and do, and how they do not say and do it. As you get better and better at it you will appear to be empathic, and in most ways you are. But instead of some unexplainable ESP, it is you simply using your eyes and ears in ways others simply do not. This extra skill/ability will allow you to find out things about candidates that other recruiters will miss. These things will allow you to hire the best candidates, learn how to work with the hardest teammates and managers and simply make your life easier. After all, it is always easier dealing with people when you understand them, and these skills will give you insights that others will not have.

Complacency is a Recruiters Worst Enemy

Recruiters can suffer from the same negative effects of success that anyone else does. The main issue is complacency. Sometimes a recruiter or anyone who has great success can become complacent. Sit back on their laurels so to speak. Sometimes with recruiters, it can also happen because they think they know the business they support to well, or they have a lot of candidates in the pipe. However the reality is there is no such thing as too many because inevitably, some will fall off for varying reasons such as; change their minds, fail tech screen, cannot relo, HM changes their mind, etc... Then you are stuck with not enough because you become complacent.

In some cases, the complacency comes from thinking they have so much experience they know it all. Trust me you do not. I have over 15 years in staffing and I still attend at least 2 webinars on staffing, recruiting, Boolean searches, social media, etc. every month. Trust me you never know it all, there is always something new, sometimes it is directly related to staffing, sometimes it is Program management, sometimes time management. There is always something you can learn, some new knowledge, skill or tool you can add to your skills set to make yourself better.

The point now matters how good you think you are, there is always someone better. No matter how successful you are there is always someone more successful or a way for you to be more successful. Do not become complacent. Continue to strive to be better or I can guarantee you someone, and maybe even the whole industry will pass you by.

The Secret Acronym Language of Staffing

So like all vocations and companies, staffing has their own language of sorts. Most of it revolves around acronyms and abbreviations. I know in the US Army alone they have a "book of Acronyms". Actually more like a set of books, in that the "book" is composed of 28 books each book being 400+ pages of acronyms.

Well, the Staffing one is not that big. Today I am going to state what some of the more common acronyms stand for. For a definition, simply put the following string in your search engine: define XXX were X equals what the acronym stands for, example define "Affirmative Action", you will get: " Affirmative Action-program to stop discrimination: a policy or program aimed at countering discrimination against minorities and women, especially in employment and education." This should work with most of the acronyms.

On to the acronyms!

AA- Affirmative Action

AAP- Affirmative Action Plan

ACIR- Advanced Certified Internet Recruiter

ADA- Americans with Disabilities ACT

ADEA- Age Discrimination Employment ACT

AIRS- Advance Internet Recruiting Strategy

AM- Account Manager

AMR- Account Management Recruiter

ASA- Addition by Subtraction by Addition (See my blogs)

ASA- American Staffing Association

ASK- Abilities, Skills and Knowledge

ATS- Applicant Tracking System

BFOQs- Bona Fide Occupational Qualifications

BIO- Biography

BQs- Basic Qualifications

BTOS- Business, Targeted, Open Door, Sequential Interviewing system

Cand- Candidate

CBT- Computer Based Training

CDR- Certified Diversity Recruiter

CERS- Certified Employee Retention Specialist

CGR- Candidate Generation Recruiter

CIR- Certified Internet Recruiter

Comp- Compensation

CPC- Certified Personnel Consultant

CPRW- Certified Professional Résumé Writer

CSP- Certified Staffing Professional

CSSR- Certified Social Sourcing Certification

CTS- Certified Temporary-Staffing Specialists

CV- Curriculum Vitae

DOL- Department of Labor

ECRE- Elite Certified Recruitment Expert

EEO- Equal Employment Opportunity

EPA- Equal Pay Act

ER- Employee Referral

GPHR- Global Professional In Human Resources

HM- Hiring Manager

HMCS- Hiring Manager Closer to Staffing (See my blogs)

HR- Human Resources

HRIS- Human Resources Information System

Int- Interview

ITSM- Information Technology Staffing Management

JD- Job Description

KPI- Key Performance Indicators

KSAOs- Knowledge, Skills, Ability and Other Characteristics

KSAs- Knowledge, Skills, and Abilities

KSI- Key Success Indicators

MBO- Management by Objectives

NAPS- National Association of Personnel Services

NCRW- Nationally Certified Resume Writer

NHSA- National Healthcare Staffing Association

NWRA - Northwest Recruiters Association

OFCCP- Office of Federal Contract Compliance Program

PARWCC- Professional Association of Résumé Writers & Career Coaches

PDA- Pregnancy Discrimination Act

PHR- Professional In Human Resources

PRC- Physician Recruiting Consultant

PRC- Professional Recruiter Certification

Relo- relocation

Res- Resume

RR or Req review - Requirements Review- a review of a soon to be open headcount

SAT - Systems Approach to Training

SC - Staffing Consultant

SEO- Search Engine Optimization

SHRM- Society for Human Resource Management

SLA-Service Level Agreement

SMS- Social Media Staffing or Web2.0

SP- Staffing Professional

SPHR- Senior Professional In Human Resources

STL- Staffing Thought Leader

Tech or Tech screen- a technical interview.

TS- Talent Sourcer

TSC- Technical Services Certified

TSO- Total Staffing Optimization (See my blogs)

UGESP- Uniformed Guidelines of Employee Selection Procedures

URM- Underrepresented Minority

Of course, there is a great deal more, these are just some of the common ones.

"People Aggregator", the Catch-all That Needs to Stop

The term "People Aggregator" has become a catch-all for a lot of different kinds of tools. So much so it is being overused, misused and is time to get it straight.

So before we go on please let me make it very very clear, Entelo, Gild and Talent Bin is not the only People Aggregators out there. Do not get me wrong they are very very good, I use them, but they are not the only ones. Once you understand what a People Aggregator is and how many different kinds there are you will open yourself up to a whole new world of aggregators
People Aggregators by definition are tools that allow you to bring information and sometimes save information on people in one place. People Aggregators fall under several subcategories, listed below.

ATS/CRM- yes ATS/CRM systems are People Aggregators. Examples Taleo, ICIMS, PC Recruiter, etc.

Job Boards with resume databases – yes these too are People Aggregators. Examples are Monster, CareerBuilder, Dice etc.

Social Aggregators- these are tools that aggregate information about a person and brings it to you. Examples are 360social, Leaf, Riffle, Peoplegraph, Prophet, Falcon, etc.

Scraping Aggregators-these are tools that scrape sites and allow you to bring in that scraped information to a site for data manipulation. Examples Zip profile, Capture, etc.

Network Aggregators- these are your networking/social sites. After all, they are all about aggregating people, they just rely on the people to add the info rather than finding it for themselves. Examples are LinkedIn, Facebook, G+

Combined Aggregators-these is tools that do a multiple of things. The example they might allow you to save a profile and also bring in other information into the profile from other sites. Examples Connect6, Conectifier, Archively, etc.

Hopefully, this will help make things more clear and we can start being specific when we talk about People Aggregators.

Pattern-Based Recruiting

The other day I was speaking to a friend of mine in the Data world. He was talking about data, pattern recognition and the like. It got me thinking and realizing we as staffing professionals do a fair amount of pattern recognition, or at least we should be. I mean let's think about it if you have an open position. It's a position your company has hired for before and may even have people already doing it or has done it and succeeded. Why wouldn't we do an analysis of all the people who have been successful in this role and see what the patterns are, or for that matter do the same thing for those that failed to see if there is any pattern there as well? This could only help us to target the best candidates.

For instance what if out of 10 people who have filled the role successfully we found out 8 came from an Ivy League school, or 8 had worked at Microsoft before. This would tell us people from those schools or who have worked at Microsoft are more likely to succeed than others. You can use any one of a number of data points. Data point such as; type or degree, college, last company, years of experience, geographical location, and more can all tell us the whys of success and failure. Now I know what you're thinking how is geo-relevant. Well, what if you do your analysis and discover 90% of the people from the Midwest that move to take this job to fail. Let's remember that is a huge culture shock and that could be why they fail.
The concept here is simple past success or failures can help determine future success or failures.

All you simply need to do is analyze the data and identify the patterns.
So where to start, first, you identify an equal number of successes and failures in a position, then identify the data to analyze. Then you pull the data and look for the patterns. Pretty simple concept huh?

Take some time but in the end could help improve your quality of hire, length of hire and time to hire as you will have a better idea what it takes to succeed.

How to ask Questions to Determine a Candidates Integrity & Honesty!!

Determining the honesty and integrity of a candidate is very tough. Especially if done over the phone. Below are some ideas and questions you can ask that will help you to determine a candidate's honesty and integrity:

- Describe a time when you spoke up even though it was unpopular.
- Describe a time when you admitted a mistake to a co-worker.
- How do you earn the trust of others?
- Would those you've worked with describe you as a person of integrity? Why did they reach that conclusion?
- Can you describe a time at work when you brought bad news to your manager?
- Discuss a time when your integrity was challenged. How did you handle it?
- Have you ever experienced a loss for doing what was right?
- What is the worst professional obstacle you've ever had to face and how has it helped you to grow?
- What three skills will you need to continue to develop to be "the best you can be?"

Each of these questions is designed to determine the honesty, integrity, and ability of a candidate to take a stand.

The Art of Resume Sourcing

I would like to focus on the art of searching for resumes on the Internet. Spending time sourcing for candidates on the Internet is just as important as posting a great job. Sourcing is probably more valuable than posting because it is proactive and gives the Recruiter control over who applies.

Sourcing is a skill that is not easy to master. Why? Simple, answer is because no search is usually ever the same. You could have several Recruiters search the same database yielding completely different results. Why? Another simple answer, because there is no set formula for successful sourcing. Understanding that no search is the same, I have listed a few tried and true sourcing tricks that will help you in your searching. I'm sure you may have a couple tricks of your own up your sleeve (and I would love to hear them) but here is a few that work well:

Understand *EXACTLY* what you are searching FOR– This usually goes without saying but is usually the first thing to trip up your sourcing efforts. At my company, the Recruiter's motto is "my search is only as good as the order taken". Taking a good order or requisition from your hiring managers is imperative. Do some homework and research ahead of time to make sure you are asking all the right questions.

Translate the Job Description to a Resume – Keywords are crucial when sourcing, so understanding what kind of keywords will be on the resumes you need is vital. Too many times the job description uses minute detail keywords that your candidates would not bother with on their resume. Don't let one keyword throw off your entire search. Consider the words a candidate would use on their resume and use those for your search.

Start Small – Don't waste time sifting through tons of resumes. Use a narrow search string to identify no more than 50 resumes. If you have to click through more than 8 resumes to identify 1 fit then your search string should be altered. An ideal string is one in which every other resume click through identifies a match. By focusing on a strong search string you are eliminating wasted time clicking through unqualified resumes. Broaden your search as you go to make sure you have identified every possible candidate match.

Double Check Your Search String – Sometimes these strings get very long and it's easy to make a grammatical mistake! If you are surprised at the lack of results in your search it could very well be because there is a mistake in your search string.

Consider the Search "A Work In Progress" – Mold and shape your search by pulling out good keywords identified from those resumes that were a match. These words may not even be skill sets. For instance, in one case my search string for a Technical Project Manager used words like "led", "team" and "lead" because I had identified a pattern in the resumes that were qualified. Keep a sharp eye and look for similarities in the words used in resumes to change your search string as you go.

Don't Stop Short – Too many times we try a couple search strings, contact a few candidates and stop there. Make sure you use all available search strings to pull and contact as many candidates as you can. It's a numbers game to take advantage of the existing search and time.

Please be Patient – Sourcing takes a lot of time and attention to detail. Don't start a search at the end of the day; you'll forget where you left off. Don't answer your phone or accept visitors during your sourcing time; you'll lose your focus. Don't expect instant results right away. It takes time and experience to be strong at sourcing and it does not come instantaneously.

Hopefully, you have found these tips and tricks helpful. Remember, sourcing successfully is an art that takes research, time and attention to detail. Good luck!

Hiring Managers do not Understand Recruiting

As a rule, most hiring managers do not understand recruiting. They think all we do is look at Monster or Hotjobs (which was just bought by monster) or the other databases and find people with no problems. They do not understand the amount of work that goes into the sourcing part of recruiting. One way I have found that has helped me educate the hiring manager is to arrange sourcing sessions with them. Make an appointment to meet with them and talk about the opening and source. You will be amazed at how different they will think once they sit with you for 30 minutes and your source. I have done it many times and they come away with a new appreciation and even admiration for what we do. You will find it strengthens your relationship with the hiring manager and by default will make recruiting easier.

No School like the Old School

In today's modern age staffing world, we are overwhelmed with the sheer number of recruiting and sourcing tools, add-ons, extensions, apps, and more. In today's staffing world there is a tool for everything. However, despite this, we still struggle to find, connect with, and hire the best and brightest. Now there are numerous reasons for this, economic climate, location, skill population, company reputation, and more. What is so interesting is, perhaps one of the biggest issues is the staffing professionals themselves. Because of all these tools, too many staffing professionals were never taught the "old school" skills and abilities that allowed us to do our jobs before all the tools came. Chief amongst them is communications. Not just talking but Listening and writing as well. The ability to write a good job description, the ability to talk to a potential candidate, and perhaps most importantly the ability to listen that's right, *listen is the key*. Listening is one of the most important old-school skills we have. If you listen properly, you can almost always fund the motivating hot buttons for a candidate and then use them to get what you need. Communication is an "old school" skill that should be still used now and always. Why the hell are you even asking a question if you don't want to hear the answer?

Now please keep in mind the "old school" skills I am talking about are not just communication. They are using Boolean, X-raying, sleuthing, and the phone. With all of the tools that are out there, far too many staffing professionals rely on email as their primary and in a lot of cases the only way to communicate. Pick up the phone, call someone you might be surprised by the responses you get. For those of you who are LinkedIn users but do not have a LinkedIn recruiter account try x-raying in, but make sure you are not signed into your LinkedIn account. This will allow you to see pretty much everyone and more info that you would with your non recruiter account. X-raying works with almost every site so it is not just LinkedIn that you can do this with AND its free!

The new age of staffing tools is upon us, but forgetting the "old school" skills is a huge mistake that no staffing professional can afford to make in this candidate tight market. Remember there is no school like the old school.

Sourcers/Recruiters Checklist

So I have been asked a lot about how I keep things straight and do what I do. I always refer them to my PM and words to recruiting by posts. So this post is additional to those, consisting of a simple checklist.

Opening identified:

1.   Meeting with the hiring manager(HM) to write JD (if applicable)
2.   Research on what JD says, example resumes found and brought to intake meeting
3.   Intake meeting to discuss opening:
a.   Go over JD and resumes
b.   Discuss nice to have, have to haves etc.
c.   Target candidates and companies
d.   Salary, location etc.
e.   Referrals
f.   Anything else
g.   Complete and agree upon SLA
4.   Update JD if needed and post
5.   Send out meeting notes and SLA for approval
6.   Research to go beyond the basics
7.   Create and implement a sourcing plan (some of this will be determined during the   research stage)
a.   Low hanging fruit
1.   Internal DB, referrals
2.   Monster, dice, CareerBuilder, indeed, Craigslist etc.
b.   Mid hanging fruit
1.   Linkedin, Beknown, professional social sites. etc.
2.   networking
c.   High hanging fruit
1.   User groups, newsgroups
2.   Conferences, White papers, Patents, etc.
3.   Targeted companies
4.   Free Boolean searches, doc finders, IMetasearch, Copernic etc.

5. Social searches using tools like IceRocket, twitter, blogdigger, github, code.google, search-it, google+, etc.
6. Deep web tools like Foca, maltego etc.
8. Contacting candidates
a. Email

1. Low hanging- talk about opportunity first, always ask to connect on social sites and if
they know anyone.

2. Mid hanging- talk about their expertise and wanting to ask questions, always ask to
connect and if they know anyone

3. High hanging- socialize first
    8. Interview/vet
    9. Present those that pass, disposition those that fail
    10. Set up tech screens

4.. Set up face to face (F2F) interviews for those that pass tech screen, disposition those
    that fail

5. Discuss results of F2F
    a. Put together and make offers to those who passed F2F.
    b. Disposition those who fail

6. Offer
    a. If offer accepted update system, close position
    b. If offer decline disposition and return to process

NOTE STEPS 7-12 AND 13B CONTINUE UNTIL STEP 13A IS COMPLETE AND POSITION IS FILLED OR PULLED

Note in some cases there might be an added step or 2 or some steps listed might be combined but these are the essentials

Bring the heart back to Staffing

I wrote this 3 years ago, and when I reread it I realized it applies now more than ever.

So "The heart of Rock and Roll" as Huey Lewis sang, is still beating. The question is how is the heart of staffing? From the things, I have seen and heard I seriously question if the "heart of staffing" even exists anymore.

What I mean by the "heart of Staffing" is the reason we do it, the way we do it, the way we handle ourselves with people etc. I sometimes think because of social media, ATS, HRIS, and metrics, etc. we forgot what it is like to be …human, what it is like to be a candidate, and hiring manager, heck I think some forget what it is like to be a staffing professional.

What brought this up was listening to the way a recruiter I meant was talking to a prospective candidate for the first time. They were quick, cold, callous, uncaring, and basically acted like the candidate was wasting their time. The interesting part was the candidate was perfect for the position. It made me start listening and watching what other staffing professionals do and say, not to just applicants but other recruiters and hiring managers. While they were, for the most part, cordial, and polite, there was no zest, no sense of caring. They were almost robotic, there were "PC" but nothing else, there was no heart.

One thing I have learned in my years in staffing is you have to have heart, you have to want to do this because you love it, you have to want to talk to candidates to not just see if they have the skills you need but to see what they are all about, what kind of person are they, what is in their hearts. You need to talk with hiring managers like they are more than just an annoying person who wants something, but more as a person who needs your help. We are in the time of "Social Media" trust me everyone knows when you treated someone bad when you stopped caring when you stopped having a heart.

What I am saying is start acting human, start using your heart. Start remembering what it is like in the other person shoes, start remembering the way you want to be treated and remember the way you treat someone now will come back to you, the only question is will it be for the good or bad. Remember we are in the age of "Social Staffing" so having a heart is important.

Lean Staffing Part 1 Process

Over the last few weeks, I have been asked about the process I use when dealing with issues like process, organization, and staffing tools. The process is called "Lean Staffing", now while this is similar to the lean in lean manufacturing or the lean used in project management, the terminology is a little different, instead of expenditures, we have processes, procedures, metrics, people, tools etc. So for the purposes of staffing Lean means: taking a process, procedures, metrics, organization, tools and breaking it down into their core components, metrics, procedures and removing any redundancies, combining any like steps, removing or improving on shortcomings inability, cutting down time allowances, selecting the correct tools, and removing any wasted communications. Or perhaps the best definition of lean that crosses all boundaries is simply put; doing more with less.

This will be the first in a 3 part series where we discuss using Lean Staffing to help with our processes, organizational structure, and tools. It consists of 3 types of analyses; Lean staffing process analysis, Lean Staffing Organizational Analysis, and Lean Staffing tools analysis, These analyses can be done at any time and multiple times on several different levels. Meaning you can do a Lean staffing Process analysis of the process as a whole and or the specific work process of an individual. First up Processes.

The way I approach this is to research, and observe each and every step in the staffing process being used, and the time allowed to perform them. I then create a line chart being sure to incorporate every step, every communication point, any system involved and how it is used. From there it is a simple matter of crossing off the redundancies, combining like steps and removing any needless or wasted communications.

For instance, at one company I worked the staffing process from position needs assessments to hire had over 30 steps, and over 50 communications links. After analyzing the process and creating my line chart, I was able to take the 30 steps and narrow it down to

15, and take the 50+ communication links and narrow them down to 18, and take time allowances and cut them in half. Long story short we had a process that was shorter, easier and quicker.

Now in this post, we spoke about "Lean Staffing" as it relates to the process of staffing. Over the next few posts, I will explain how "Lean Staffing" works with Organizational structure, tools, and more.

Lean Staffing Part 2 Organization

In part 1 you read about using Lean Staffing to improve your process. This time we are going to talk about Lean Staffing to help your organizational structure.

So in order to utilize Lean Staffing to improve your organizational structure you first need to determine what staffing model you are using. Are you using a mono model-meaning full cycle staffing, are you using the di-model -splitting the staffing function into 2 parts, the tri-model -splitting the staffing function into 3 parts, or some other model.

Once you have determined that, you need to do a Lean Staffing organizational analysis, of the metrics used and measured over a 5 year period by each function of the model. Meaning for the mono model it will not matter much, but for di-model or tri-model each split or added function will have its own metrics and numbers. An example is in a di-model you would have the sourcing metrics and numbers for the source and the recruiter (account management) metrics and numbers for the recruiter position. You want to do a 5-year analysis and find out the averages of all the metrics and numbers for each function. Then list them, then find the avg numbers for each person in the organization over their tenure in the organization, according to their roles. Once you have done that you have a list of people and whether they fall above or below your avg line or Mendoza line.

So now you know who is not getting it down and who is. Here is where Lean Staffing really kicks in. Now that you have all that info, if you find out what your goals are for the upcoming year you can determine how many people you need, and in which roles to fulfill then, presuming you only keep or hire those who can at least obtain the averages as outlined in the above paragraph. Odds are you will not need as many people and therefore will be able to carry a leaner team, or you will find out through further Lean Staffing analysis there is a process, procedure or tool getting in the way of your people not just meeting the goals but destroying them.

Example: you currently have a team of 7 in a mono-model or full cycle, the past 5-year avg shows that each person should hire an avg of 30 people in a year. However when you look at your current 7 people their averages over their time at the company show you have 2 avg 30, 3 avg 35 and 2 avg 10.

Now what you need to do is find out the who, what, why, were, and how of the numbers. Part of this is going to be doing a Lean Staffing process analysis and or a Lean Staffing tools analysis, you may find out the process or tools are causing everyone to be less productive then they should be. You may find out that everyone should be able to hire 40 and you do not need 7 people and therefore can do more with less, or keep all 7 and destroy the goals.

If nothing comes from doing either the lean staffing process or tools analysis then utilize Lean Staffing process analysis with regards to the way each person below the Mendoza line is doing their job and see if there is wasted time, lack of training or processes that are hindering their ability to hire more.
If after all that, there is no doubt it is the individuals in the roles, you let them go and find 1 person who can meet the avg and therefore meet the goals, or you hire 2 and destroy your goals.

The point is if you keep using Lean staffing you will find the answer and be able to do more with less. Now in this post, we spoke about "Lean Staffing" as it relates to the organization of staffing. Next up is tools.

Lean Staffing Part 3 Tools

In part 2 you read about Lean staffing as it relates to the organization and how you can do more with less and or find out why more is not being done. This time we will talk about Lean Staffing as it relates to tools.

Tools are a huge part of staffing, whether it is an ATS, HRIS, Sourcing tools, Job Boards, Social media tools or whatever they are huge.

The question is how do we determine which ones to use. The first thing you need to do is determine is which you already have and what they do and which new ones are appropriate for the industry you are staffing for. Then you need to determine what kind of avenues you want to use to find, attract and contact prospective candidates as well as post your openings.

Once you have done all of that you make a block diagram showing what each tool do, and then start crossing out tools missing things you need until you narrow it down to the 1 tool that gives you what you need, if there is more than 1 than look at the cost as the final determining factor.

Example"

Tools 1	Tool 2	Tool 3	Tool 4
Tool 5	Tool 6		
ATS	ATS	ATS	ATS
ATS	ATS		
JP	JP	JP	JP
	JP		
	SM	SM	
SM			
Mobile	Mobile	Mobile	
	TC		TC
TC	TC		

JP= job posting   SM=Social Media   TC=Talent Community

Now in the example, the only tool that has everything you are looking for is Tool 2. Now keep in mind this was a simple example, but you get the point, Now in some cases, you might decide to live without some things, or already have tools that needed to be added to the analysis. In the end, the goal is to find 1 tool that can do everything, and if not one as few as possible as the more you use the more it costs and the more time it takes to use. Also, keep in mind this was a simple example there are many variables you might want to add to the list of things to chart in your analysis comparing tools.

Now one would think after that you are done but not so fast. Now you have to see how that tool interacts with the tools you have that are needed, for example, your ATS interacts with finance for when you make hires. To do this just use simple Lean Staffing tool analysis, by putting a box for every system used in the staffing lifecycle from seeing if you need someone to onboarding. Then create all the connection threads, add in your new tool and possible connection threads, and then start getting rid of the redundancies in both function and connections. Sound familiar? It should it is very similar to the Lean Staffing process analysis. Except here you are dealing with a process dealing with tools, not a process of dealing with people. When you are done you should know what needs to go, what needs to be implemented and in the end have one lean set of tools for staffing.

Well, there you have it, *Lean Staffing*.

Is Fit a Deterrent to Innovation?

All you hear when you talk to companies is fit, the right fit, fits in with the team, etc. The problem is fit, can and usually does mean ensuring that the people you bring in, are of similar type, thoughts, skills, demeanor, and attitude. The problem with that is it goes totally against what it takes for innovation to happen. Innovation is what happens when people with different backgrounds, views, demeanor, skills, and attitudes come together to solve a problem or improve on something. So you can see how these 2 concepts can go against each other and in fact how it makes "Fit" a deterrent to innovation. Of course that said let me qualify what I mean here, I mean when the term or idea of "Fit" is taken to the extreme, when we do not leave open any room for differences to be a good thing. While this may be not happening a lot it does happen sometimes. Sometimes people just get so caught up in the "Fit", they forget differences can be a good thing too.

New Breed of Recruiter huh?

Over the last few months, I have been inundated with questions both email and over the phone, from the "new breed" of recruiters. Now I use the term "new breed" to describe what is a growing number of recruiters who, well basically are not really recruiters but dart throwers. What I mean by "dart Throwers" is they do not really read your resume or even do a proper search, they just throw emails out hoping to get a hit and hoping it is the right hit.

What I mean is with the advent of LinkedIn; many recruiters do nothing but mine LinkedIn and their own DB. Then they send emails out hoping for someone to reply. What's worse is they are really not reading our resumes or profiles. I have received 10 emails this week alone from recruiters asking if I were interested in a job, but the job they talked about is not even close to what I do. Last I checked I am not a Surveyor, and nothing in my profile would indicate I am.

The reason I am writing this is in an attempt to get companies and recruiters to listen. To get back to using some old school skills and techniques like Boolean strings, x-raying, research, and actually matching someone's profile to a job and not just throw darts. To train your recruiters on how to be a recruiter, how to read and create a job description, how to pick the right skills out and put together a sourcing strategy to find what you need to find, how to properly contact the right candidates, and engage them, and so much more. Basically, train them how to be real recruiters. Over the next few blogs, I will talk about the skills, techniques you need to train your recruiters in to become real recruiters that can add value, and not dart throwers. #truestory

The Future of Social Job Descriptions and Branding is DIAL!!

In the world of Social media, we as staffing professionals need to be smart. We need to find ways to reach out to our target audience within the confines of the social media sphere. Social media is mainly 3 styles of communication; written (twitter etc.), pictorial (Pinterest etc.), and video (Vimeo etc.). The question is how do we do it? How do we run a campaign that can hit all 3, and also accomplish the idea of finding possible candidates and branding ourselves correctly?

The answer is DIAL, which stands for "Day in a Life". Basically what DIAL is, is a way in which you utilize word, pictures, and video to explain what a "day in a Life" of a given person performing a given job at a company. Think of a "day in the Life" as a written, almost diary-like a statement of what a typical day in the life of a professional at your company is like. For example, you would write what a day in a life of a PM (program manager) is at a given company. You would perhaps have a picture of a meeting they might attain, a snapshot of their calendar of a given day, showing meetings, showing appointment that might show not only work but work-life balance. You might even record a message from this PM about what his job is about. In the end, you make it clear you are looking for others like this PM. Now obviously you will want to choose a PM who is well connected, lots of LinkedIn connections, Twitter followers, someone who blogs to maximize things.

Once all the above is done, you can now post on LinkedIn, post on your website, use the pictures for Pinterest, and the video for Vimeo and more. It is a complete social staffing strategy, that brands the company, brands the job, and does it in the social sphere.

It's a Small World After all, and the Pyramids

I know what you are thinking, what does a Disney song; have to do with the Pyramids? Well, the connection is really very simple.

Let's start with the pyramids or the premise of a pyramid. There is an old adage, if you tell a secret to someone, they will tell someone else, who will tell 2 more who will each tell 2 more, and before you know it everyone knows about the secret. Worse what you told the first person and what the last people were told will not be the same. The secret will grow legs and turn into some monster that is so far from the truth, that it becomes out of control. This is the "pyramid principle" of communication. Each conversation builds onto another conversation and grows, like a pyramid.

Now let's say you are a staffing professional, and you speak to a potential candidate and you treat them like a piece of meat. What do you think they are going to tell others? Trust me it will not be good. Of course, given the number of candidates around, you figure so what no worries. Well here is where the "it's a small world after all" comes to get you.

Good people in a particular vocation or with particular skills tend to gravitate toward others of like vocations and skills. Heck, the whole social community phenomenon is built on this premise. Well, let's say you treat a C# developer like a piece of meat and they, for good reason, get upset. Who do you think they are going to tell? The answer, others they communicate with, in most cases more C# developers, and of course, those developers will tell others and so on, and on, and on until an entire community thinks you treat people like meat. Guess what, now no one in that community will talk with you, and eventually it will grow even bigger.

Now perhaps you can see how "It's a small world after all and the Pyramids" are connected. A staffing professional's reputation, how they treat their candidates, co-workers, etc. is going to dictate how successful they might be in the future. Because people will talk, treat them well, and everyone will be open and available, treat them bad, and eventually you will find yourself on the outside looking in.

Technical Testing When and how to do it!!!

Within the staffing community, Hiring teams (HT, this consists of the Hiring manager, and possibly first and second level interviewers) and businesses themselves there has always been controversy over how do you determine the expertise level of a candidate. Interviews, technical testing, reference checks, and more are all tools that can be used. Some staffing professionals (SP), and companies rely purely on one of the aforementioned tools. (Please keep in mind this applies mainly to corporate staffing)

In reality, it should not be any one thing. It should be a combination, some people are not good test takers, but can perform the job way above and beyond. The key is to remember an interview, a test, a resume, a reference check, social media checking, are all parts of the puzzle that needs to be done to get the full picture. That is not to say you must do them all to make a decision. However the more you know the better decision you can make.

As it relates to testing it is very important to remember that you do not make the test too long, and that you administer it at the right time or you will lose potential candidates who do not want to waste time taking a long test when they have not been given the opportunity to talk to anyone from the HT to ensure they are interested. A SP can only get a candidate so interested then the HT must help.

An example of a process that incorporates all of these tools is below (this is a shortened version and not all inclusive just an example)

1.   Decision made to make a hire

2.   JD wrote and posted

3.   Sourcing happens

4. A candidate found from sourcing or applies (this means resume are screened to determine first level fit) and are screened by staffing professional. These screens include talking with the candidate, and social media check (this includes; blogs, LinkedIn recommendation, SP network check, etc.).

5. Results presented to HT, in some cases, it is a simple thumbs up.

6. Candidates who are chosen for next steps talk with first level HT interviewer, who spends 5-10 minutes asking general questions to gain more info, usually, these are general technical questions. Reason for this is also to allow the candidates to ask more question about the job, group, etc. (remember the candidates are interviewing the company hiring as well as we are interviewing them.)

7. The decision is made to go on to the next step or not.

8. If the decision is to move on to next step then SP sends a 5-10 question technical test. If not SP lets the candidate know

9. Results of the technical test are put together with SP screen, first level HT screen, resume, social media check, and any other info to determine if face to face interviews should happen. The key here is no one thing should make a candidate a go or a no. If the candidate did well on the phone with the first level HT interviewer but only did okay on the tech test you might want to still bring them in.

Of course, you might be able to delete a step here and there or add as needed, but you get the idea. The point is to ensure any testing is done at the right time, is not too long and is only a piece of the puzzle used to determine next steps.

How Many Staffing Professionals are too Many?

Is the answer to an increase in staffing needs always to add more recruiters, or sourcers? Do we really think the answer is always to add more? Is more really better? The answer is not always more but perhaps better, or perhaps educating what you have, or even breaking apart the Staffing Lifecycle (SLC) into parts and assigning different parts to different people, i.e. sourcing, calling, etc.

What if you have a team of 4, 2 account management recruiters (AMR) and 2 sourcers? If you are having problems filling your openings perhaps the answer is who is doing what. Perhaps one of the AMR's would make better sourcers and vice versa. I was speaking to a friend of mine who manages a staffing team of 6. He was talking to me about the fact they are not filling enough positions fast enough. I asked him what he thought the problem was? He said he was not sure, but the management wanted to add more recruiters. I said okay that is one way to go, but perhaps before you do you should do an analysis; find out were in the SLC the issue is. He agreed and we talked about how he should do it. Long story short after doing it, he discovered the issue was 2 fold. One a lack of training and 2 not taking advantage of what he had. What he had was 3 strong AMR's and 3 strong sourcers. However since all were full-cycle, he was not taking advantage of their strengths. So a simple switch to an AMR and sourcer model, and 3 months later all was good.

The point is before you go adding people look at what you have, look at their skills maybe the answer to your problem is not adding more, but utilizing the skills of what you have.

Not I, but WE !!

I was recently speaking to some recruiters at a particular company. A few had known of me from my Microsoft (MS) days. One of them asked me how I made the big hirer numbers I did at MS. I told them I didn't. They looked at me shocked. I went on to explain, that yes the numbers were made, but that it took a team to do it. I could not have made those numbers without the interview coordinators taking care of the interviews I submitted. I could not have done it without my recruiting coordinators support and help, or my teams, or my hiring managers and their teams, or HR, or Legal or compensation, or any one of a number of people who all played a part in my being able to get those large numbers. They seem amazed that I would say that, I went on to explain it is not about the "I" it is about the "we". I then referred them to the book "Conscious Business" by Fred Kofman. All that said the point is do not forget all the people it took for you or anyone to succeed, make it about the "we", appreciate the people who help you.

The Forgotten Secret Weapons to Optimization

What are these "Secret weapon" you wonder; A Dictionary and Thesaurus. That is right probably two of the oldest books around is the secret weapon. Now first let's not think of Dictionaries and Thesaurus's as only the old books on our bookshelves. I am talking about any dictionary; the standard, online, technical, etc.. Any book or website that defines things is by definition a dictionary. The same goes for a Thesaurus.

Now how can these two types of resources help us, as staffing professionals? Well in the age of the search engine, the ages were you need to think of any way you can possibly write something and have it mean the same thing. The age of "Search Engine Optimization", both as a standard search engine, a job board or a database, the ability to come up with all the different ways a person might search for something or the words they might put on their resume or in a document can help us find hidden gems.

Example let's look up a resume in a thesaurus:

- You get-Curriculum Viate, Vita, CV, Synopsis, Abstract, Precis, Work History, Biography, summary, Bio etc..

- So now let's do a quick search in google

- inurl:resume yields over 5,710,000 results.

- inurl:work history yields over 4,510 and yes some of those results are what we would call resumes.

- inurl:"work history" yields 15,100 results and again some are what we would call resumes.

So you can see how just looking up the word resume in a thesaurus, gave us other ideas on how to search. Also, remember I used just a standard thesaurus. There are all types and all will give you other words that mean the same thing.

Let's look at another example; you need a tester, well if you look up testing in a technical thesaurus you will see a lot of interesting words used to mean testing, such as "reverse engineering". If you search on testing you will get a certain number of hits, you search on "reverse engineering" you will get a certain number of hits, but you will get a large percentage that will not be the same. Of course, the same principle works with search strings, job descriptions, resume writing, blogging etc..

Basically, all we are doing by using these age-old tools, in all their varied forms are doing a type of optimization. Whether it is a job description, search string or resume writing the idea is to use as many possible words, and phrases that mean the same thing as what we want, in the event someone out there, and they will, uses them also.

Recruiters and Falsehoods

Falsehoods that is the nice way to say lies in any industry and ours is no different. The act of stating falsehoods, or lies, is way more prevalent in staffing than we would like to think. Some staffing professionals (SPs) seem to feel whatever it takes to land the candidate is ok. Now, this is much more prevalent in the contract world than the corporate world, But it does happen in both. Things as simple as, we can pay you this much when you know you cannot. Are statements that are made that are false. Eventually, it does come back to haunt you. As an SP, our business is people, and if we have a bad reputation, as someone that cannot be trusted, then that reputation will get out and will grow. Now if it just stayed centered on that one SP it would be fine and a trusted pint. But the reality is as it grows, as other SPs say things that are not true, and their reputation goes bad and gets around, the reputation tends to become generalized. It only takes a few bad apples to spoil the whole bunch. This means while maybe less than 10% of SPs use falsehoods to land the candidate, that less than 10% and their reputation will be what people think of when they think of Staffing Professionals. It is like the NBA referees, only 2-3 were linked to fixing and such, But even though it was only 2-3 out of 100, the fans, players, and even the league questioned all referees. The bad reputation of a few can become the reputation of all, even the good ones. The moral here is before an SP states something they know is false, remember it will be found out, it will get around, and it will not be just your reputation that suffers, but the reputation of all SPs, and the industry itself.

The Devaluing of Sourcers

The devaluing of sourcers has become a sticking point of late. I have seen companies offer $15 an hour and less for a sourcer. Worse they actually find sourcers to take it. So the question is, why? Do companies really think Sourcing is easy? Could it be a product of the current economic climate, the high number of available candidates, or do the companies feel anyone can source? Or is it that there are so many job board and database "sourcers" that they have devalued sourcing as a whole. I mean we all know some of these sourcers, who only use the job boards, and only look for candidates in the company database. They do nothing with Boolean searches, or social media, or any of the other ways real sourcers search. Let's be real the Sourcing part of Staffing is arguably the most important and the hardest. So why does it appear sourcing is being devalued.

I believe it is a little bit of everything. I do believe due to the economic climate, some companies think they can get a good sourcer for next to nothing. I also believe that due to the large numbers of available candidates some companies feel anyone can do it. I also believe part of it is the number of "job Board" and "database" sourcers that are out there. Now, what can be done about it? That answer is simple, wait. Sooner or later the crème always rises to the top, and those that cannot truly source will fail, and companies will realize going cheap, does not get the job done. In fact, it can load falsehoods, remember that to help them support the idea that sourcing is a less needed function for their recruiters when it really is not. Let me explain with an example.

ABC Company hires a sourcer with little experience for $15 an hour. The sourcer tries to find candidates using some traditional methods. The sourcer finds a few people but the recruiter and manager are not overly impressed as the people that are called are not interested in the role or interview and blow it. That is not the sourcers fault but yet since they do not know what a sourcer really does the person is blamed and let go or reprimanded. All for what a basic service worker should be making at a restaurant.

There is no argument here that would hold water at all. Sourcers are information gatherers that bring not only people to the table but all sorts of information about people, companies, industries, etc? I think that is worth a hell of a lot more than $15, don't you?

Staffing Professional, Recruiter, Sourcer and More

So one thing I have read a lot about, and see the terms used allot are the terms/title; Staffing Professional, Recruiter, Source, etc.. But there have not been any real definition to them. So after doing a lot of research here is a simplistic version of what I have come up with. Please remember these are a generalization, I am sure there are one-offs, and places were the lines blur allot.

Staffing Professional (SP) = A professional who has mastered all parts of staffing, who can source, screen, account manager, job description(JD) writer, interviewer, functional analyst, PM, negotiate, report generator, consulting with Hiring managers, be a closer, internal hiring, career development/counseling, resume writing, trainer, HRIS/ATS and more (simplistic, as each part has multiple subparts with multiple tools and methods used)) all this makeup or are needed to fully understand the Staffing Lifecycle (SLC). These people are normally associated with corporate staffing. Of course, while they have mastered all parts of staffing that does not mean they perform all parts, all the time. They might have help with some. But in the end, they have mastered it all.

Recruiter = they have mastered most parts of the SLC, but this title is mostly associated with agency or consulting company positions. They have mastered all parts of the recruiting, from a different perspective than a Staffing Professional, as the people they hire are usually put on assignment in another company or at least working at another company. So the way a JD might write is different, the closing is different, as for account management- in this case, it could range from none to candidate account management to client account management, etc... Usually, there is no consulting with the hiring managers here as you are there to get in, fill the opening and on to the next. The consulting or long-term relationship is usually built by the account manager. Note I said usually as there are full-service recruiters or full desk as they are known. These recruiters do it all, but again from a consulting or contract perspective. Not saying one is better than the other just different.

Also, of course, just because they have mastered it all, does not mean they do it all, or do not have help.

As you can see Recruiter and Staffing Professional are very close to the same thing. Just a matter of what industry you are in.

Sourcer = This is someone whose job it is to find potential candidates. This function can be just finding to finding and screening of candidates. They very rarely write JDs, rarely have any account management responsibilities. They are purely sourcers, or researchers as some call them. This title is universal across corporate, consulting and contracting. All industries use this title and it is arguably the most important and the toughest to find top-notch sourcers. Of course, most Staffing Professionals usually are top notch sourcers as well.

Screener= This is someone whose sole function is just to screen candidates. Usually, they are either doing simple HR screens or reading from a script.

JD writer = as the name implies they write JDs. believe it or not, there is even a certification for it. This actually falls under the tech writing vertical but is a part of Staffing and Recruiting.

Talent Engagement = these are very similar to the Staffing Professional, and usually, use in the corporate world. In the case of Talent Engagement, they will usually also be involved with internal hiring, but not the same as a staffing professional. They go into more depth, in that they not only look at the here and now , but the future. Looking at internal talent to see where and when they might be ready for the next assignment. Now there are other names for this role, but let's stick with this one, as there are way too many to go through.

Employment Specialist = These tend to be more about finding jobs for people then finding people for jobs. Think of it as reverse recruiting. This happens to allot in the military, colleges, etc...

Account manager = these tend to be the people who have direct contact with the client or hiring manager. In the case of contract companies, they can also manager the onsite temps.

Now let's look at some of the functions not already described in the titles above:

PM = a good SP will treat each opening like a project, and as such will be able to effectively manage their time, resources, and complete the Staffing Life Cycle (SLC) with great success.

Report Generator = well any good SP knows keeping, generating reports is what allows them to show there worth, and what they are doing.

Functional Analyst (FA)= simply a good SP is an FA, meaning they know how to get the requirements and information they need to be successful.

Negotiator and Closer = A Good SP knows how to negotiate with both clients and candidates. Of course, you have to be a closer in order to be a negotiator

JD writer = any SP worth their salt knows how to write a good, effective, and well marketable JD.

Interviewer = again you cannot be a good SP without knowing how to interview, both your candidates and your HMs.

Screener = Different from interviewing screening is what a good SP does of any resume to determine if the candidate is a possible match prior to interviewing. This can also include simple HR screens and screening that is done over the phone or email

Consultant = This is one of the biggest functions of an SP and one of the biggest differences between an SP and a recruiter. An SP is a consultant to their hiring manager, teaching them, helping them to navigate the murky waters of the hiring process.

Other words used in some titles are personnel and career.

Well there you have it, a simplistic version of who is who and what it what, again this is not all-inclusive. Does not mean there are not some line blurring or overlap, missing titles, or one-offs, this is just a generalization based on the research I have done.

The Few, the Proud, the Looking, and why you should hire them

Yes, we are talking about the military. Every year thousands of these proud warriors get out and face an uncertain future. Not knowing what they should do.

However, there are some things everyone should keep in mind, concerning the military. There are some skills or rather ideals, and things they learn that make them ideal employees. These people live and breathe the ideals of; loyalty, honor, hard work, determination, going beyond, and sacrifice. In their world, if you do not live by these ideals, people die. Of course, in most cases, they come equipped with a lot of education benefits, a lot of relevant training, and a lot of heart and desire.

So if you want to have an employee who will give their all, will never give up, be loyal, honorable, and be the kind of employee you could be proud of, hire an ex-military person, and watch them, not just get the job done, but get it done right, done quickly and watch them make you look good.

The BIG T Word; Transition from Military to Civilian

For those transitioning out of the military into the civilian world, it may be very stressful and downright scary. How do you take all you learned and accomplished, done and transfer it to a civilian occupation. It is tough and very daunting, but it can be done. I am ex-military and I did it. Below outlines some of the things you will need to get and do, and some resources available to help.

First use the ACAP (Army Career Alumni Program) or transition serves office on your installation. They will have a lot of great resources.

Next, gather all your training certificates, your reviews, your 2–1, make sure you get an AARTS transcript (http://aarts.army.mil/Order.htm). Also, ensure you have all the various manuals that describe your MOS. Also, make sure you have access to a computer and can access the DOL website. There will be a list of occupations and what each does. Also below are some other useful resources:

http://www.careerkokua.org/ce/mi/employment/article.cfm?id=19

http://careers.stateuniversity.com/pages/100000329/Resumes-Members-Military-Transitioning-Civilian-Careers.html

http://www.careeronestop.org/MilitaryTransition/

http://www.quintcareers.com/former_military.html

http://www.rileyguide.com/vets.html

Naturally, there are more, you may use this simple search string to find them: "transition AND military AND civilian" or "transitioning from military to civilian." Put either into your web search and you will see a lot.

Once you have all that, you can start to figure out what it is you are trained to do in the civilian world and write a resume that is geared to that vocation. For resume writing, go to this link http://www.recruitingblogs.com/profiles/blogs/your-resume-the-key-to-new it will explain how to write a resume that will get the job done. You may also get resumes writing tips from some of the links listed above under resources. Also, go to the link below for tips on job-hunting

http://www.recruitingblogs.com/profiles/blogs/the-job-of-finding-a-job.

The biggest thing is figuring out what you can and want to do, and then go for it. For instance if you were a 75B, you probably qualify for some jobs within HR. Do not forget to use your educational benefits, to gain new or more training or education to enhance yourself.

Above all, remember you are not in this alone. There are groups and organizations out there that can help, VFW, for example. In fact, if you have any questions or need any help contact me at star434343@comcast.net and I will be happy to help you.

Chapter 6

The
Summation

Final Thoughts from Derek "DZ" Zeller and Dean Da Costa

I have been a fan and a friend of Dean's for some time now and was honored to be asked by him to help put this book of thoughts together. This is a compilation of online posts that Dean has done over time and a nice compilation of my choosing. Yeah, my mind is like the Joker on meth but hey it was his choice so...

Most people do not know Dean is multi-lingual, so, at times; his verbiage is tough to understand. However, that is not a crutch it is amazing as I have placed many linguists over the years who speak multiple languages and have told me that English was the most complicated one they had to learn. Hell, I struggle with it and it is kind of the only one I know how to speak. If you have ever tried to write, like really write, you know the struggles one can endure especially when you are trying to extoll knowledge to novices; for free no less.

I have amused that Dean asked me of all people to edit a book for him. My editors are laughing as well and I am sure that there are imperfections within this book. However, Dean and I liked it and frankly, I think we need to get past the so-called Kings English and go the route of Mr. Clemons and speak the way the world is now just like he did in some of the greatest books in the history of snarkiness and misunderstanding in the world today. Yes, you did pay for this book, not much really, just a bunch of pennies put together, a couple of beers or coffees I suppose. However, there is knowledge here, hard thoughts for you to think about and gems of knowledge from a man who has spent years learning and sharing with our community.

The term "Thought Leader" gets tossed around in so many industries, especially ours I would surmise. It strokes egos, I suppose, and there are many of the old guards that like that and profit from it. Dean, like me, are those who do the work, did the work, paid our dues and we are looking, as many of us are to lift up the community, a compilation of souls, men and women, who have formed our own mythical Sisyphus pushing that boulder up the mountain. We would love to hear from you, teach you, learn from you, or just have a cup of tea OR whiskey. #truestory

Join us won't you?

Deans Final Thoughts

I got my first real taste of HR and Staffing in the military. Upon exiting the military as a disabled vet I found it difficult to find a job. In most cases companies only talk to me to check a box. I remember very clearly to this day my first phone interview. I was told by the recruiter they were only talking to me to check a box, and that everything I learned and did in the military is worthless in the civilian world.

That was well over 20 years ago, and a lot has changed. I got lucky, I got a chance form an agency whose recruiting lead really liked military. The problem was they also did not know how to train so I was thrown to the wolves. The exact wording was "here is your deck and computer figure it out" no training no nothing. Right then I realized my Military background would, could and did see me through. I worked hard to learn what I know and to succeed. The other thing I realized is no one should be put in that position. None should be thrown to the wolves.

That is why I with Derek's help wrote this book. That is why he and I and many, many others talk at Sourcecon, Talent42, ERE, and other conferences and does webinars as well as joins organizations such as ATAP (Association of Talent Acquisition Professionals), NWRA (North West Recruiting Association), Sourcing 7 and others. We do it give back, to help, to leave the staffing world better than it was when we joined. We want to ensure that no one is told to sit at a computer and hear the words 'Figure it out". It has been my pleasure and honor to do whatever I can to help those in the industry, to make the staffing world better. I am also truly blessed to have so many friends who support each other in every way, and who have welcomed with open arms my son Jeremy who is also a sourcer, and already giving back as he too writes blogs, and speaks at Sourcecon and Sourcing 7. We are in a wonderful time in the recruiting and sourcing world at a time when so many willingly give of themselves to help our community As a token of my knowledge of tools I have added what I feel are what I think the top tools out there are right now on the next page. I hoped you enjoyed the book and happy sourcing!

Top Tool Recommendations

Keep in mind this list is always changing and updating. Tool come and go, however **to** keep update check out my web page on tools at:

http://thesearchauthority.weebly.com/tools.html

- **Chrome Productivity-**Extensity, tidy bookmarks, context, Temporary Bookmarks, APPJump, ChromeWebstore, One Tab, Find My Bookmarks
- **Search Productivity-** EZlink preview, Google Enhancement Suite, Multiple File Download, Docs Online Viewer, Google When?, Web Page Sticky Notes
- **Scraper-**Dataminer/Scraper, Copylead, Email Exporter, WebClipDrop, Web Scraper
- **Social Info/People Aggregator/Email Finding-**Email Qualifier, Contactout, Lusha, Toofr, Nymeria, People Search, Snovio, JobJet, Seekout Sourcing Assistant, TalentSnap, Uproc, HOLA, Context Scout, Connectifier Social Links, 360Social, **Prophet**
- **Complete Sourcing Solution-** Hiretual, Seekout, Whoknows, Engage Talent
- **Boolean/xray-** Source hub, Bool, SourcingLab, Talentsonar
- **Linkedin-** LeadIQ, LOXO, most people aggregators
- **Facebook-** Search is Back, Intelligence Search, most aggregators
- **G+-**Search Ext G+, most aggregators
- **Twitter-** Riffle, PropelIQ, Twitter Advance Search, most aggregators
- **Github-** Hikido, Get Discovered, GitHub Email Reveal, GitHub emails revealer, Hirables, GitAwards, most aggregators
- **Gmail/Email-** Full contact, Clearbitconnect, Assistant.io , Zenprospector, Accompany,
- **Gmail/Email Tracking-** Geotrack, Bananatag, Boomerang, Criptext, Evolutics

- **Email with Video- Free Video Email for Gmail, Wiind**
- **Competitive Intel/Intel – Datanyze, Fedger, Rethinklabs, inDoors - Glassdoor Integrator for Linkedin, Recap. Work -DOL, Linkedin, Glassdoor, Owler, Lead essentials, Talismantic, FYI, GlobalEdge, Accquired, Levels, DeepSense, Seekout**
- **Writing tools(emails, jds etc)- Textio,, Mosaic Track, JobLint, Crystal, Readability, Spam, DeepSense**
- **Search – Sales Search, Social Geek, Wayback machine, millionshort, Advangle**
- **Sourcing tools/sites- ContactCloud, Talismatic, Seekout, Zensourcer, LOXO AI, Whoknows, Engage Talent**
- **EXTRA= Google Sheets With (Numerous Addons) Blockspring using Full Contact, Hunter + (to many to list), Wholi**
- **Email – email-format.com, A/B Testing, , Trinsly**
- **Security /Maintenance- Touch VPN, MyPermissions, Lastpass, Ghostery, Free Proxy, 360 Internet Protection, ADBlock PLus**
- **Social- Bitly, TweetDeckLauncher, FB Notifications, G+ Notifications, Yoono, AddThis**
- **Misc- Easy URL Params, URL Monster, Grammerly, Xendo, Zip-Codes, AppWise, Google Translate, IP Whois,**
- **Communications- Google Hangouts, Zoom, Uber, Zipwhip**
- **Free ATS/CRM- CRM for Gmail, Streak CRM for Gmail, HubSpot, LOXO,**
- **OSINT- Open Source Intelligence, MaltegoCe**
- **YOUR BRAIIN!!**
  Some fit into multiple categories